Working Papers
Chapters 14-26

Accounting 25e

Carl S. Warren
Professor Emeritus of Accounting
University of Georgia, Athens

James M. Reeve
Professor Emeritus of Accounting
University of Tennessee, Knoxville

Jonathan E. Duchac
Professor of Accounting
Wake Forest University

D1275586

SOUTH-WESTERN
CENGAGE Learning·

Australia · Brazil · Japan · Korea · Mexico · Singapore · Spain · United Kingdom · United States

For product information and technology assistance, contact us at **Cengage Learning Academic Resource Center, 1-800-423-0563**.

For permission to use material from this text or product, submit all requests online at **www.cengage.com/permissions**. Further permissions questions can be emailed to **permissionrequest@cengage.com**.

ISBN-13: 978-1-285-07313-2
ISBN-10: 1-285-07313-4

South-Western, Cengage Learning
5191 Natorp Boulevard
Mason, OH 45040
USA

Cengage Learning is a leading provider of customized learning solutions with office locations around the globe, including Singapore, the United Kingdom, Australia, Mexico, Brazil, and Japan. Locate your local office at: **international.cengage.com/region**.

Cengage Learning products are represented in Canada by Nelson Education, Ltd.

For your course and learning solutions, visit **www.cengage.com**.

Purchase any of our products at your local college store or at our preferred online store **www.CengageBrain.com**.

Printed in the United States of America
1 2 3 4 5 6 7   15 14 13 12

CONTENTS

The working papers include problem-specific forms for preparing solutions for Exercises, A&B Problems, the Continuing Problem, and the Comprehensive Problems from the textbook. These forms, with preprinted headings, provide a structure for the problems, which will help you get started and save you time.

Based on students' testimonials and instructors' feedback, the forms in the working papers have been streamlined to make them simpler to use and to better reflect the changing environment of business. For example, the vertical rules that separated digits of numbers entered into journals, ledgers, and statements have been removed, making it easier to write in numbers. Also, the formats of the end-of-period spreadsheet (work sheet) and several other forms have been updated to better resemble actual electronic spreadsheets.

Note that when entering whole amounts into the forms, your instructor will direct you on whether to include a decimal point and zeroes (e.g., 100.00) or to omit those (e.g., 100).

APPENDIX 2 EXERCISE 14-24

a. 1. through 3.

JOURNAL

	DATE		DESCRIPTION	POST. REF.	DEBIT	CREDIT	
1							1
2							2
3							3
4							4
5							5
6							6
7							7
8							8
9							9
10							10
11							11
12							12
13							13
14							14
15							15

b.

c. _____

_____

_____

_____

_____

_____

_____

APPENDIX 1 AND 2 EXERCISE 14-25

a. through d.

APPENDIX 1 AND 2 EXERCISE 14-26

a. through d.

This Page Not Used.

PROBLEM 14-1 ___   14 5 8 9 10 13 16 21   P3a

1.

	Plan 1	Plan 2	Plan 3
Earnings before interest and income tax	$	$	$
Deduct: Interest on bonds...............................			
Income before income tax................................	$	$	$
Deduct: Income tax.......................................			
Net income	$	$	$
Deduct: Dividends on preferred stock			
Available for dividends on common stock.............	$	$	$
Divided by: Shares of common stock outstanding			
Earnings per share on common stock	$	$	$

2.

	Plan 1	Plan 2	Plan 3
Earnings before interest and income tax	$	$	$
Deduct: Interest on bonds...............................			
Income before income tax................................	$	$	$
Deduct: Income tax.......................................			
Net income	$	$	$
Deduct: Dividends on preferred stock			
Available for dividends on common stock.............	$	$	$
Divided by: Shares of common stock outstanding			
Earnings per share on common stock	$	$	$

PROBLEM 14-1 ___, Concluded

3. _____

PROBLEM 14-2 ___

1. and 2.

JOURNAL   PAGE

	DATE		DESCRIPTION	POST. REF.	DEBIT	CREDIT	
1							1
2							2
3							3
4							4
5							5
6							6
7							7
8							8
9							9
10							10
11							11
12							12
13							13
14							14
15							15

3. _____

4. _____

_____

_____

_____

_____

5.

This Page Not Used.

© 2014 Cengage Learning. All Rights Reserved. May not be scanned, copied or duplicated, or posted to a publicly accessible website, in whole or in part.

Name _____

PROBLEM 14-4 ___

1.

JOURNAL

PAGE

	DATE		DESCRIPTION	POST. REF.	DEBIT	CREDIT	
1							1
2							2
3							3
4							4
5							5
6							6
7							7
8							8
9							9
10							10
11							11
12							12
13							13
14							14
15							15
16							16
17							17
18							18
19							19
20							20
21							21
22							22
23							23
24							24
25							25
26							26
27							27
28							28
29							29
30							30
31							31
32							32
33							33
34							34
35							35

PROBLEM 14-4 ___, Continued

JOURNAL

	DATE		DESCRIPTION	POST. REF.	DEBIT	CREDIT	
1							1
2							2
3							3
4							4
5							5
6							6
7							7
8							8
9							9
10							10
11							11
12							12
13							13
14							14
15							15
16							16
17							17
18							18
19							19
20							20
21							21
22							22
23							23
24							24
25							25
26							26
27							27
28							28
29							29
30							30
31							31
32							32
33							33
34							34
35							35
36							36

PROBLEM 14-4 ___, Concluded

2. (a) 2014: _____

   (b) 2015: _____

3.

This Page Not Used.

APPENDIX 1 AND 2 PROBLEM 14-5 ___

1. and 2.

JOURNAL   PAGE

	DATE		DESCRIPTION	POST. REF.	DEBIT	CREDIT	
1							1
2							2
3							3
4							4
5							5
6							6
7							7
8							8
9							9
10							10
11							11
12							12
13							13
14							14
15							15
16							16
17							17
18							18
19							19
20							20

3. _____

This Page Not Used.

APPENDIX 1 AND 2 PROBLEM 14-6 ___

1. and 2.

JOURNAL

	DATE		DESCRIPTION	POST. REF.	DEBIT	CREDIT	
1							1
2							2
3							3
4							4
5							5
6							6
7							7
8							8
9							9
10							10
11							11
12							12
13							13
14							14
15							15
16							16
17							17
18							18
19							19
20							20

3. _____

This Page Not Used.

EXERCISE 15-1

a. through d.

JOURNAL

	DATE		DESCRIPTION	POST. REF.	DEBIT	CREDIT	
1							1
2							2
3							3
4							4
5							5
6							6
7							7
8							8
9							9
10							10
11							11
12							12
13							13
14							14
15							15
16							16
17							17
18							18
19							19
20							20
21							21
22							22
23							23
24							24
25							25

EXERCISE 15-2

a. through d.

JOURNAL

PAGE

	DATE		DESCRIPTION	POST. REF.	DEBIT	CREDIT	
1							1
2							2
3							3
4							4
5							5
6							6
7							7
8							8
9							9
10							10
11							11
12							12
13							13
14							14
15							15
16							16
17							17
18							18
19							19
20							20
21							21
22							22
23							23
24							24
25							25

EXERCISE 15-3

a. through d.

JOURNAL

	DATE		DESCRIPTION	POST. REF.	DEBIT	CREDIT	
1							1
2							2
3							3
4							4
5							5
6							6
7							7
8							8
9							9
10							10
11							11
12							12
13							13
14							14
15							15
16							16
17							17
18							18
19							19
20							20
21							21
22							22
23							23
24							24
25							25
26							26
27							27
28							28
29							29
30							30
31							31
32							32
33							33
34							34
35							35

EXERCISE 15-4

a. and b.

JOURNAL   PAGE

	DATE	DESCRIPTION	POST. REF.	DEBIT	CREDIT	
1						1
2						2
3						3
4						4
5						5
6						6
7						7
8						8
9						9
10						10
11						11
12						12
13						13
14						14
15						15
16						16
17						17
18						18
19						19
20						20
21						21
22						22
23						23
24						24
25						25
26						26
27						27
28						28
29						29
30						30
31						31
32						32
33						33
34						34
35						35

EXERCISE 15-5

EXERCISE 15-6

a., b., and c.

JOURNAL

PAGE

	DATE		DESCRIPTION	POST. REF.	DEBIT	CREDIT	
1							1
2							2
3							3
4							4
5							5
6							6
7							7
8							8
9							9
10							10
11							11
12							12
13							13
14							14
15							15
16							16
17							17
18							18

EXERCISE 15-7

JOURNAL

	DATE		DESCRIPTION	POST. REF.	DEBIT	CREDIT	
1							1
2							2
3							3
4							4
5							5
6							6
7							7
8							8
9							9
10							10
11							11
12							12
13							13
14							14
15							15
16							16
17							17
18							18

EXERCISE 15-8

JOURNAL

	DATE		DESCRIPTION	POST. REF.	DEBIT	CREDIT	
1							1
2							2
3							3
4							4
5							5
6							6
7							7
8							8
9							9
10							10
11							11
12							12
13							13
14							14
15							15
16							16
17							17
18							18
19							19
20							20
21							21
22							22
23							23
24							24
25							25
26							26
27							27
28							28
29							29
30							30
31							31
32							32
33							33
34							34
35							35
36							36

EXERCISE 15-9

JOURNAL

	DATE	DESCRIPTION	POST. REF.	DEBIT	CREDIT	
1						1
2						2
3						3
4						4
5						5
6						6
7						7
8						8
9						9
10						10
11						11
12						12
13						13
14						14
15						15
16						16
17						17
18						18
19						19
20						20
21						21
22						22
23						23
24						24
25						25
26						26
27						27
28						28
29						29
30						30
31						31
32						32
33						33
34						34
35						35
36						36

EXERCISE 15-10

a.

		DATE	DESCRIPTION	POST. REF.	DEBIT	CREDIT	
1							1
2							2
3							3
4							4
5							5
6							6
7							7
8							8
9							9
10							10
11							11
12							12

JOURNAL   PAGE

b. _____
_____
_____
_____
_____
_____
_____
_____
_____

EXERCISE 15-11

a.

JOURNAL   PAGE

	DATE	DESCRIPTION	POST. REF.	DEBIT	CREDIT	
1						1
2						2
3						3
4						4
5						5
6						6
7						7
8						8
9						9
10						10
11						11
12						12
13						13
14						14
15						15
16						16
17						17
18						18
19						19
20						20

b.

EXERCISE 15-12

a.

JOURNAL

PAGE

	DATE		DESCRIPTION	POST. REF.	DEBIT	CREDIT	
1							1
2							2
3							3
4							4
5							5
6							6
7							7
8							8
9							9
10							10
11							11
12							12
13							13
14							14
15							15

b.

EXERCISE 15-12, Concluded

c. _____

_____

_____

_____

_____

_____

_____

_____

_____

_____

_____

_____

_____

_____

EXERCISE 15-13

_____

_____

_____

_____

_____

_____

_____

_____

_____

EXERCISE 15-14

JED Capital Inc.

Selected Income Statement Items

For the Years Ended December 31, 2014 and 2015

	2014	2015
Operating income	a. _____	e. _____
Unrealized gain (loss)	b. _____	$(11,000)
Net income	c. _____	28,000

JED Capital Inc.

Selected Balance Sheet Items

December 31, 2013, 2014, and 2015

	Dec. 31, 2013	Dec. 31, 2014	Dec. 31, 2015
Trading investments, at cost	$144,000	$168,000	$205,000
Valuation allowance for investments	(12,000)	17,000	g. _____
Trading investments, at fair value	d. _____	f. _____	h. _____
Retained earnings	$210,000	$245,000	i. _____

EXERCISE 15-15

a.

	JOURNAL				PAGE	
	DATE	DESCRIPTION	POST. REF.	DEBIT	CREDIT	
1						1
2						2
3						3
4						4
5						5
6						6
7						7
8						8
9						9
10						10
11						11
12						12
13						13
14						14
15						15

b. _____

_____

_____

_____

_____

_____

EXERCISE 15-16

a. and b.

	JOURNAL				PAGE

	DATE		DESCRIPTION	POST. REF.	DEBIT	CREDIT	
1							1
2							2
3							3
4							4
5							5
6							6
7							7
8							8
9							9
10							10
11							11
12							12
13							13
14							14
15							15
16							16
17							17
18							18

EXERCISE 15-17

a.

		JOURNAL				PAGE

	DATE	DESCRIPTION	POST. REF.	DEBIT	CREDIT	
1						1
2						2
3						3
4						4

Computations:

b. _____

_____

_____

_____

_____

_____

_____

_____

EXERCISE 15-18

a.

b.

EXERCISE 15-19

Highland Industries Inc.
Selected Income Statement Items
For the Years Ended December 31, 2014 and 2015

	2014	2015
Operating income	a. _____	g. _____
Gain (loss) from sale of investments	$7,500	$(12,000)
Net income	b. _____	(15,000)

Highland Industries Inc.
Selected Balance Sheet Items
December 31, 2013, 2014, and 2015

	Dec. 31, 2013	Dec. 31, 2014	Dec. 31, 2015
Assets			
Available-for-sale investments, at cost	$ 90,000	$ 86,000	$102,000
Valuation allowance for available-for-sale investments	12,000	(11,000)	h. _____
Available-for-sale investments, at fair value	c. _____	e. _____	i. _____
Stockholders' Equity			
Unrealized gain (loss) on available-for-sale investments	d. _____	f. _____	(16,400)
Retained earnings	$175,400	$220,000	j. _____

EXERCISE 15-20

a.

JOURNAL   PAGE

	DATE		DESCRIPTION	POST. REF.	DEBIT	CREDIT	
1							1
2							2
3							3
4							4
5							5
6							6
7							7
8							8
9							9
10							10
11							11
12							12
13							13
14							14
15							15

b. _____

_____

_____

_____

_____

_____

_____

EXERCISE 15-21

a. 1. and 2.

JOURNAL   PAGE

	DATE		DESCRIPTION	POST. REF.	DEBIT	CREDIT	
1							1
2							2
3							3
4							4
5							5
6							6
7							7
8							8
9							9
10							10
11							11
12							12
13							13
14							14
15							15

b. _____

_____

_____

_____

_____

_____

_____

_____

_____

_____

EXERCISE 15-22

a.

	JOURNAL				PAGE

	DATE		DESCRIPTION	POST. REF.	DEBIT	CREDIT	
1							1
2							2
3							3
4							4
5							5
6							6
7							7

Computations:

b. _____

_____

_____

_____

_____

_____

_____

_____

_____

_____

EXERCISE 15-23

a.

	Balance Sheet (selected items)		

b.

	Balance Sheet (selected items)		

EXERCISE 15-24

Balance Sheet (selected Stockholders' Equity items)		

EXERCISE 15-25

_____

_____

_____

_____

_____

EXERCISE 15-26

a. Year 1: Dividend Yield: _____

   Year 2: Dividend Yield: _____

b. _____

_____

_____

_____

_____

_____

_____

_____

EXERCISE 15-27

APPENDIX EXERCISE 15-28

APPENDIX EXERCISE 15-29

PROBLEM 15-1 ___

1.

JOURNAL   PAGE

	DATE		DESCRIPTION	POST. REF.	DEBIT	CREDIT	
1							1
2							2
3							3
4							4
5							5
6							6
7							7
8							8
9							9
10							10
11							11
12							12
13							13
14							14
15							15
16							16
17							17
18							18
19							19
20							20
21							21
22							22
23							23
24							24
25							25
26							26
27							27
28							28
29							29
30							30
31							31
32							32
33							33
34							34
35							35

PROBLEM 15-1 ___, Continued

JOURNAL   PAGE

	DATE		DESCRIPTION	POST. REF.	DEBIT	CREDIT	
1							1
2							2
3							3
4							4
5							5
6							6
7							7
8							8
9							9
10							10
11							11
12							12
13							13
14							14
15							15
16							16
17							17
18							18
19							19
20							20
21							21
22							22
23							23
24							24
25							25
26							26
27							27
28							28
29							29
30							30
31							31
32							32
33							33
34							34
35							35
36							36

PROBLEM 15-1 ___ , Concluded

2. _____

This Page Not Used.

PROBLEM 15-2 ___

1.

JOURNAL PAGE

	DATE		DESCRIPTION	POST. REF.	DEBIT	CREDIT	
1							1
2							2
3							3
4							4
5							5
6							6
7							7
8							8
9							9
10							10
11							11
12							12
13							13
14							14
15							15
16							16
17							17
18							18
19							19
20							20
21							21
22							22
23							23
24							24

Calculations:

PROBLEM 15-2 ___, Continued

JOURNAL

PAGE

	DATE	DESCRIPTION	POST. REF.	DEBIT	CREDIT	
1						1
2						2
3						3
4						4
5						5
6						6
7						7
8						8
9						9
10						10
11						11
12						12
13						13
14						14
15						15
16						16
17						17
18						18
19						19
20						20
21						21
22						22
23						23
24						24
25						25
26						26
27						27
28						28
29						29
30						30
31						31
32						32
33						33
34						34
35						35
36						36

PROBLEM 15-2 ____, Concluded

2.

Balance Sheet (selected items)

3. _____

_____

_____

_____

_____

_____

_____

_____

_____

_____

_____

This Page Not Used.

PROBLEM 15-3 ___

1.

JOURNAL   PAGE

	DATE		DESCRIPTION	POST. REF.	DEBIT	CREDIT	
1							1
2							2
3							3
4							4
5							5
6							6
7							7
8							8
9							9
10							10
11							11
12							12
13							13
14							14
15							15
16							16
17							17
18							18
19							19
20							20
21							21
22							22
23							23
24							24
25							25
26							26
27							27
28							28
29							29
30							30
31							31
32							32
33							33
34							34
35							35

PROBLEM 15-3 ___, Continued

JOURNAL

PAGE

	DATE		DESCRIPTION	POST. REF.	DEBIT	CREDIT	
1							1
2							2
3							3
4							4
5							5
6							6
7							7
8							8
9							9
10							10
11							11
12							12
13							13
14							14
15							15
16							16
17							17
18							18
19							19
20							20
21							21
22							22
23							23
24							24
25							25
26							26
27							27
28							28
29							29
30							30
31							31
32							32
33							33
34							34
35							35
36							36

PROBLEM 15-3 ___, Concluded

2.

	Balance Sheet (selected items)		

This Page Not Used.

PROBLEM 15-4 ___

a. _____

b. _____

c. _____

d. _____

e. _____

f. _____

g. _____

h. _____

i. _____

Calculations:

PROBLEM 15-4 ____, Continued

Completed comparative unclassified balance sheet (optional):

Balance Sheet

	DEC. 31, 2015	DEC. 31, 2014

PROBLEM 15-4 ___, Concluded

Calculations:

_____

_____

_____

_____

_____

_____

_____

_____

_____

This Page Not Used.

EXERCISE 16-16

a.

Cash Flows from Operating Activities		

b. _____

_____

_____

_____

_____

_____

_____

_____

EXERCISE 16-17

a.

Statement of Cash Flows		

EXERCISE 16-17, Concluded

b. _____

_____

_____

_____

_____

_____

_____

_____

_____

_____

_____

_____

_____

_____

_____

_____

_____

_____

_____

_____

EXERCISE 16-18

EXERCISE 16-18, Continued

(Optional)

Statement of Cash Flows

EXERCISE 16-18, Concluded

Statement of Cash Flows (continued)

EXERCISE 16-19

a.

b.

c. _____

_____

_____

_____

EXERCISE 16-20

EXERCISE 16-21

a.

b.

EXERCISE 16-22

a.

Computations:

EXERCISE 16-22, Concluded

b. _____

_____

_____

_____

_____

_____

_____

_____

_____

_____

_____

_____

EXERCISE 16-23

Computations:

EXERCISE 16-24

a.

b. _____

_____

_____

_____

_____

_____

EXERCISE 16-25

a.

	RECENT FISCAL YEAR END (all numbers in thousands)

EXERCISE 16-25, Concluded

b. _____

_____

_____

_____

_____

_____

c. _____

_____

_____

_____

_____

EXERCISE 16-26

This Page Not Used.

PROBLEM 16-2 B

Statement of Cash Flows

Cash			
AC Receiv			
Inv			
PP expenses			
Land			
Bldgs			
Acc Dep – Building			
Machinery and equipment			
Accum Dep – Machinery & equip			
Patents			
Acc payable			
Div payable			
Sal payable			
Mortgage Payable Due 2017			
Bonds payable			
Common stock, $5 par			
Paid in capital - excess of issue price or par			
Retained earnings			

PROBLEM 16-2 ___, Continued

Statement of Cash Flows (continued)

PROBLEM 16-2 ___, Continued

The use of this form is not required unless so indicated by the instructor.

	A	B	C	D	E
1					
2		Spreadsheet (Work Sheet) for Statement of Cash Flows			
3					
4		Balance, _____	Transactions		Balance, _____
5	Account Title		Debit	Credit	
6					
7					
8					
9					
10					
11					
12					
13					
14					
15					
16					
17					
18					
19					
20					
21					
22					
23					
24					
25					
26					
27					
28					
29					
30					
31					
32					
33					
34					
35					
36					
37					
38					
39					
40					
41					
42					
43					
44					
45					

PROBLEM 16-2 ___, Concluded

	A	B	C	D	E
1					
2	Spreadsheet (Work Sheet) for Statement of Cash Flows (continued)				
3					
4	Account Title	Balance, _____	Transactions		Balance, _____
5			Debit	Credit	
6					
7					
8					
9					
10					
11					
12					
13					
14					
15					
16					
17					
18					
19					
20					
21					
22					
23					
24					
25					
26					
27					
28					
29					
30					
31					
32					
33					
34					
35					
36					
37					
38					
39					
40					
41					
42					
43					
44					
45					

PROBLEM 16-3 ___

Statement of Cash Flows			

PROBLEM 16-3 ___, Continued

Statement of Cash Flows (continued)

PROBLEM 16-3 ___, Continued

The use of this form is not required unless so indicated by the instructor.

	A	B	C	D	E
1					
2		**Spreadsheet (Work Sheet) for Statement of Cash Flows**			
3					
4		**Balance,**	**Transactions**		**Balance,**
5	**Account Title**	**_____**	**Debit**	**Credit**	**_____**
6					
7					
8					
9					
10					
11					
12					
13					
14					
15					
16					
17					
18					
19					
20					
21					
22					
23					
24					
25					
26					
27					
28					
29					
30					
31					
32					
33					
34					
35					
36					
37					
38					
39					
40					
41					
42					
43					
44					
45					

PROBLEM 16-3 ___, Concluded

	A	B	C	D	E
1					
2		Spreadsheet (Work Sheet) for Statement of Cash Flows (continued)			
3					
4		Balance, _____	Transactions		Balance, _____
5	Account Title		Debit	Credit	
6					
7					
8					
9					
10					
11					
12					
13					
14					
15					
16					
17					
18					
19					
20					
21					
22					
23					
24					
25					
26					
27					
28					
29					
30					
31					
32					
33					
34					
35					
36					
37					
38					
39					
40					
41					
42					
43					
44					
45					

PROBLEM 16-4 ___

Statement of Cash Flows

PROBLEM 16-4 ___, Concluded

Computations:

EXERCISE 17-1

a.

	2014		2013	
	AMOUNT	PERCENT	AMOUNT	PERCENT
Comparative Income Statement

b. _____

_____

_____

_____

_____

_____

_____

EXERCISE 17-2

a.

		Comparative Income Statement (in thousands of dollars)				

	CURRENT YEAR		PRIOR YEAR	
	AMOUNT	PERCENT	AMOUNT	PERCENT

EXERCISE 17-2, Concluded

b. _____

_____

_____

_____

_____

_____

_____

_____

_____

_____

_____

_____

_____

_____

_____

_____

_____

_____

_____

_____

EXERCISE 17-3

a.

	BULL RUN COMPANY		ELECTRONICS INDUSTRY AVERAGE
	AMOUNT	PERCENT	

Common-Sized Income Statement

b. _____

_____
_____
_____
_____
_____
_____
_____
_____
_____
_____

EXERCISE 17-4

Comparative Balance Sheet

	2014		2013	
	AMOUNT	PERCENT	AMOUNT	PERCENT

EXERCISE 17-5

a.

Comparative Income Statement

	2014 AMOUNT	2013 AMOUNT	INCREASE (DECREASE)	
			AMOUNT	PERCENT

EXERCISE 17-5, Concluded

b. _____

_____

_____

_____

_____

_____

_____

_____

_____

EXERCISE 17-6

a. (1) Working Capital = _____

_____

2014: _____

_____

2013: _____

_____

(2) Current Ratio = _____

_____

2014: _____

_____

2013: _____

_____

(3) Quick Ratio = _____

_____

2014: _____

_____

2013: _____

_____

b. _____

_____

_____

_____

_____

_____

EXERCISE 17-7

a. (1) Current Ratio = _____

_____

Current Year: _____

_____

Prior Year: _____

_____

(2) Quick Ratio = _____

_____

Current Year: _____

_____

Prior Year: _____

_____

b. _____

_____

_____

_____

_____

_____

_____

_____

EXERCISE 17-8

a. _____

b. _____

EXERCISE 17-9

a. (1) Accounts Receivable Turnover = _____

_____

2014: _____

_____

2013: _____

_____

(2) Number of Days' Sales in Receivables = _____

_____

2014: _____

_____

2013: _____

_____

b. _____

_____

_____

_____

_____

_____

_____

_____

_____

_____

_____

EXERCISE 17-10

a. (1) Accounts Receivable Turnover = _____

_____

Xavier: _____

_____

Lestrade: _____

_____

(2) Number of Days' Sales in Receivables = _____

_____

Xavier: _____

_____

Lestrade: _____

_____

EXERCISE 17-10, Concluded

b. _____

_____

_____

_____

_____

_____

_____

_____

EXERCISE 17-11

a. (1) Inventory Turnover = _____

_____

Current Year: _____

_____

Preceding Year: _____

_____

(2) Number of Days' Sales in Inventory = _____

_____

Current Year: _____

_____

Preceding Year: _____

_____

b. _____

_____

_____

_____

_____

_____

EXERCISE 17-12

a. **(1)** Inventory Turnover = _____

_____

Dell: _____

_____

HP: _____

_____

(2) Number of Days' Sales in Inventory = _____

_____

Dell: _____

_____

HP: _____

_____

b. _____

_____

_____

_____

_____

_____

_____

_____

_____

_____

_____

_____

_____

_____

_____

_____

EXERCISE 17-13

a. Ratio of Liabilities to Stockholders' Equity = _____

_____

Dec. 31, 2014: _____

_____

Dec. 31, 2013: _____

_____

b. Number of Times Bond Interest Charges Are Earned = _____

_____

Dec. 31, 2014: _____

_____

Dec. 31, 2013: _____

_____

c. _____

_____

_____

_____

_____

_____

EXERCISE 17-14

a. Ratio of Liabilities to Stockholders' Equity = _____

_____

Hasbro: _____

_____

Mattel, Inc.: _____

_____

b. Number of Times Interest Charges Are Earned = _____

_____

Hasbro: _____

_____

Mattel, Inc.: _____

_____

EXERCISE 17-14, Concluded

c. _____

_____

_____

_____

_____

_____

_____

_____

_____

_____

_____

EXERCISE 17-15

a. Ratio of Liabilities to Stockholders' Equity = _____

H.J. Heinz: _____

Hershey: _____

b. Ratio of Fixed Assets to Long-Term Liabilities = _____

H.J. Heinz: _____

Hershey: _____

EXERCISE 17-15, Concluded

c. _____

_____

_____

_____

_____

_____

_____

_____

_____

_____

_____

_____

_____

_____

_____

_____

_____

_____

_____

EXERCISE 17-16

a. Ratio of Net Sales to Total Assets = _____

_____

YRC Worldwide: _____

_____

Union Pacific: _____

_____

C.H. Robinson Worldwide Inc.: _____

_____

EXERCISE 17-16, Concluded

b. _____

EXERCISE 17-17

a. Rate Earned on Total Assets = _____

_____

2014: _____

_____

2013: _____

_____

Rate Earned on Stockholders' Equity = _____

_____

2014: _____

_____

2013: _____

_____

Rate Earned on Common Stockholders' Equity = _____

_____

2014: _____

_____

2013: _____

_____

b. _____

_____

_____

_____

_____

_____

_____

_____

_____

_____

EXERCISE 17-18

a. Rate Earned on Total Assets = _____

_____

Fiscal Year 3: _____

_____

Fiscal Year 2: _____

_____

b. Rate Earned on Stockholders' Equity = _____

_____

Fiscal Year 3: _____

_____

Fiscal Year 2: _____

_____

c. _____

_____

_____

_____

_____

_____

_____

_____

_____

d. _____

_____

_____

_____

_____

_____

_____

_____

_____

EXERCISE 17-19

a. Ratio of Fixed Assets to Long-Term Liabilities = _____

_____

_____

_____

_____

b. Ratio of Liabilities to Stockholders' Equity = _____

_____

_____

_____

_____

c. Ratio of Net Sales to Assets = _____

_____

_____

_____

_____

d. Rate Earned on Total Assets = _____

_____

_____

_____

_____

e. Rate Earned on Stockholders' Equity = _____

_____

_____

_____

_____

f. Rate Earned on Common Stockholders' Equity = _____

_____

_____

_____

_____

EXERCISE 17-20

a. Number of Times Bond Interest Charges Are Earned = _____

_____

_____

_____

_____

b. Number of Times Preferred Dividends Are Earned = _____

_____

_____

_____

_____

c. Earnings per Share on Common Stock = _____

_____

_____

_____

_____

d. Price-Earnings Ratio = _____

_____

_____

_____

_____

e. Dividends per Share of Common Stock = _____

_____

_____

_____

f. Dividend Yield = _____

_____

_____

_____

_____

EXERCISE 17-21

a. Earnings per Share = _____

_____

_____

_____

b. Price-Earnings Ratio = _____

_____

_____

_____

c. Dividends per Share = _____

_____

_____

_____

d. Dividend Yield = _____

_____

_____

_____

EXERCISE 17-22

a. Price-Earnings Ratio = _____

_____

Deere & Co.: _____

_____

Google: _____

_____

The Coca-Cola Company: _____

_____

_____

Dividend Yield = _____

_____

Deere & Co.: _____

_____

Google: _____

_____

The Coca-Cola Company: _____

_____

b. _____

_____

_____

_____

_____

_____

_____

_____

_____

_____

_____

_____

_____

_____

_____

_____

_____

_____

_____

APPENDIX EXERCISE 17-23

a. Earnings per share on income before extraordinary items:

Earnings Before Extraordinary Items per Share on Common Stock = _____

_____

_____

_____

_____

_____

_____

b. Earnings per Share on Common Stock = _____

_____

_____

_____

_____

APPENDIX EXERCISE 17-24

a. _____

b. _____

c. _____

d. _____

e. _____

f. _____

g. _____

APPENDIX EXERCISE 17-25

a.

Partial Income Statement		

b.

Partial Income Statement		

APPENDIX EXERCISE 17-26

a. _____

_____

_____

_____

_____

_____

b. _____

_____

_____

_____

_____

_____

_____

PROBLEM 17-3 ___

1. a. Working Capital = _____

_____

_____

_____

_____

b. Current Ratio = _____

_____

_____

_____

_____

c. Quick Ratio = _____

_____

_____

_____

_____

PROBLEM 17-3 ___, Concluded

2.

Transaction	Working Capital	Current Ratio	Quick Ratio
a.			
b.			
c.			
d.			
e.			
f.			
g.			
h.			
i.			
j.			

Supporting calculations:

Transaction	Current Assets	Quick Assets	Current Liabilities
a.			
b.			
c.			
d.			
e.			
f.			
g.			
h.			
i.			
j.			

PROBLEM 17-5 ___

1. a.

Rate Earned on Total Assets = _____

_____

2014: _____   2011: _____

_____   _____

2013: _____   2010: _____

_____   _____

2012: _____

_____

PROBLEM 17-5 ___, Continued

b.

Rate Earned on Stockholders' Equity

Year

Rate Earned on Stockholders' Equity = _____

_____

2014: _____   2011: _____

_____   _____

2013: _____   2010: _____

_____   _____

2012: _____

_____

PROBLEM 17-5 ___, Continued

c.

<table>
<tr><td></td></tr>
</table>

Number of Times Interest Charges Are Earned (vertical axis label)

Year

Number of Times Interest Charges Are Earned = _____

_____

2014: _____   2011: _____

_____   _____

2013: _____   2010: _____

_____   _____

2012: _____

_____

PROBLEM 17-5 ___, Continued

d.

Ratio of Liabilities to Stockholders' Equity (y-axis)

Year

Ratio of Liabilities to Stockholders' Equity = _____

_____

2014: _____   2011: _____

_____   _____

2013: _____   2010: _____

_____   _____

2012: _____

_____

PROBLEM 17-5 ___, Concluded

2. _____

_____

_____

_____

_____

_____

_____

_____

_____

_____

_____

_____

_____

_____

_____

_____

_____

_____

_____

This Page Not Used.

NIKE, INC., PROBLEM

1. a. through m.

	FISCAL 2010	FISCAL 2009

NIKE, INC., PROBLEM, Continued

	FISCAL 2010	FISCAL 2009

NIKE, INC., PROBLEM, Continued

	FISCAL 2010	FISCAL 2009

NIKE, INC., PROBLEM, Continued

2. a. through m.

_____
_____
_____
_____
_____
_____
_____
_____
_____
_____
_____
_____
_____
_____
_____
_____
_____
_____
_____
_____
_____
_____
_____
_____
_____
_____
_____
_____
_____
_____
_____

NIKE, INC., PROBLEM, Concluded

738

This Page Not Used.

EXERCISE 18-1

a. Steering wheel: _____

b. Salary of test driver: _____

c. Depreciation of welding equipment: _____

d. V8 automobile engine: _____

e. Wages of assembly line worker: _____

f. Steel used in body: _____

g. Tires: _____

h. Assembly machinery lubricants: _____

EXERCISE 18-2

a. Maintenance supplies: _____

b. Wages of production line employees: _____

c. Depreciation on production machinery: _____

d. Resins for soap and shampoo products: _____

e. Plant manager salary for the Clarksville, Indiana, soap plant: _____

f. Packaging materials: _____

g. Depreciation on the Morristown, Tennessee, toothpaste plant: _____

h. Wages paid to Packaging Department employees: _____

i. Scents and fragrances: _____

j. Salary of process engineers: _____

EXERCISE 18-3

a. Factory supplies used in the Danville, Kentucky, tractor tread plant: _____

b. Interest expense on debt: _____

c. Amortization of patents on new assembly process: _____

d. Steel plate: _____

e. Plant manager's salary at Aurora, Illinois, manufacturing plant: _____

f. Vice president of finance's salary: _____

g. Property taxes on the Aurora, Illinois, manufacturing plant: _____

h. Consultant fees for a study of production line employee productivity: _____

i. Sales incentive fees to dealers: _____

j. Depreciation on Peoria, Illinois, headquarters building: _____

EXERCISE 18-4

a. Depreciation on office equipment: _____

b. Property taxes on factory building and equipment: _____

c. Advertising expenses: _____

d. Sales commissions: _____

e. Salaries of distribution center personnel: _____

f. Factory supervisors' salaries: _____

g. Factory janitorial supplies: _____

h. Repairs and maintenance costs for sewing machines: _____

i. Research and development costs: _____

j. Travel costs of media relations employees: _____

k. Chief financial officer's salary: _____

l. Oil used to lubricate sewing machines: _____

m. Depreciation on sewing machines: _____

n. Utility costs for office building: _____

o. Salary of production quality control supervisor: _____

p. Fabric used during production: _____

q. Wages of sewing machine operators: _____

EXERCISE 18-5

a. _____

b. _____

c. _____

d. _____

e. _____

f. _____

g. _____

EXERCISE 18-6

a. _____

b. _____

c. _____

d. _____

e. _____

f. _____

g. _____

EXERCISE 18-7

a. Cost to lease (rent) train locomotives: _____

b. Salaries of dispatching and communications personnel: _____

c. Costs of accident cleanup: _____

d. Wages of switch and classification yard personnel: _____

e. Cost of track and bed (ballast) replacement: _____

f. Wages of train engineers: _____

g. Payroll clerk salaries: _____

h. Safety training costs: _____

i. Fuel costs: _____

j. Maintenance costs of right of way, bridges, and buildings: _____

k. Cost to lease (rent) railroad cars: _____

l. Depreciation of terminal facilities: _____

EXERCISE 18-8

1. _____

_____

_____

2. _____

_____

_____

_____

_____

_____

_____

Manufacturing Costs

EXERCISE 18-9

a.

Income Statement		

b. Inventory balances on January 31, 2014:

Materials: _____

_____

Work in Process: _____

_____

Finished Goods: _____

_____

EXERCISE 18-10

	Balance Sheet		

EXERCISE 18-11

EXERCISE 18-12

Work in process inventory, July 1	$ 19,200	$ 43,200	(e) _____
Total manufacturing costs incurred during July	134,400	(c) _____	50,400
Total manufacturing costs	(a) _____	$252,000	$58,800
Work in process inventory, July 31	28,800	57,600	(f) _____
Cost of goods manufactured	(b) _____	(d) _____	$51,600

EXERCISE 18-13

EXERCISE 18-14

Work in process inventory, November 1	$ 52,800	$ 39,600	(e) _____
Total manufacturing costs incurred during July	282,000	(c) _____	323,200
Total manufacturing costs	(a) _____	$223,200	$360,000
Work in process inventory, November 30	62,400	52,800	(f) _____
Cost of goods manufactured	(b) _____	(d) _____	$342,400

EXERCISE 18-15

a.

Statement of Cost of Goods Manufactured			

b.

EXERCISE 18-16

a., b., and c.

EXERCISE 18-17

a. through e.

PROBLEM 18-1 ___

Cost	Product Costs			Period Costs	
	Direct Materials Cost	Direct Labor Cost	Factory Overhead Cost	Selling Expense	Administrative Expense
a.					
b.					
c.					
d.					
e.					
f.					
g.					
h.					
i.					
j.					
k.					
l.					
m.					
n.					
o.					
p.					
q.					
r.					
s.					
t.					
u.					
v.					
w.					
x.					
y.					
z.					

750

This Page Not Used.

PROBLEM 18-2 ___

Cost	Product Costs			Period Costs	
	Direct Materials Cost	Direct Labor Cost	Factory Overhead Cost	Selling Expense	Administrative Expense
a.					
b.					
c.					
d.					
e.					
f.					
g.					
h.					
i.					
j.					
k.					
l.					
m.					
n.					
o.					
p.					
q.					
r.					
s.					
t.					
u.					
v.					
w.					
x.					

This Page Not Used.

PROBLEM 18-3 ___

1. _____

   _____

   _____

   _____

   _____

2.

Cost	Direct	Indirect
a.		
b.		
c.		
d.		
e.		
f.		
g.		
h.		
i.		
j.		
k.		
l.		
m.		
n.		
o.		
p.		
q.		
r.		
s.		
t.		
u.		
v.		
w.		

This Page Not Used.

PROBLEM 18-4 ___

1. _____ Company

    a. _____

    b. _____

    c. _____

    d. _____

    e. _____

    f. _____

    _____ Company

    a. _____

    b. _____

    c. _____

    d. _____

    e. _____

    f. _____

PROBLEM 18-4 ___, Continued

2.

Statement of Cost of Goods Manufactured			

PROBLEM 18-4 ___ , Concluded

3.

	Income Statement		

This Page Not Used.

PROBLEM 18-5 ___

1.

Statement of Cost of Goods Manufactured				

PROBLEM 18-5 ___ , Concluded

2.

	Income Statement		

EXERCISE 19-1

a. _____

b. _____

c. _____

d. _____

e. _____

EXERCISE 19-2

a. Cost of goods sold:

b. Direct materials cost:

c. Direct labor cost:

EXERCISE 19-3

a.

RECEIVED			ISSUED			BALANCE			
Receiving Report Number	Quantity	Unit Price	Materials Requisition Number	Quantity	Amount	Date	Quantity	Unit Price	Amount
						July 1	300	$18.00	$5,400
31	200	$20.00				July 2	_____	_____	_____
							_____	_____	_____
			106	320	_____	July 6	_____	_____	_____
37	140	32.00				July 12	_____	_____	_____
							_____	_____	_____
			115	200	_____	July 21	_____	_____	_____

b. _____

_____

c.

JOURNAL   PAGE

	DATE		DESCRIPTION	POST. REF.	DEBIT	CREDIT	
1							1
2							2
3							3

d. _____

_____

_____

_____

_____

_____

EXERCISE 19-4

JOURNAL   PAGE

	DATE		DESCRIPTION	POST. REF.	DEBIT	CREDIT	
1							1
2							2
3							3
4							4

EXERCISE 19-5

a. and b.

JOURNAL   PAGE

	DATE		DESCRIPTION	POST. REF.	DEBIT	CREDIT	
1							1
2							2
3							3
4							4
5							5
6							6
7							7
8							8

c.

	Fabric	Polyester Filling	Lumber	Glue

EXERCISE 19-6

JOURNAL   PAGE

	DATE		DESCRIPTION	POST. REF.	DEBIT	CREDIT	
1							1
2							2
3							3
4							4

EXERCISE 19-7

a.

JOURNAL   PAGE

	DATE		DESCRIPTION	POST. REF.	DEBIT	CREDIT	
1							1
2							2
3							3
4							4

Supporting calculations:

_____

b. _____

_____

_____

_____

_____

EXERCISE 19-11

a. _____

b. _____

c. _____

EXERCISE 19-12

a.

| | JOURNAL | | | PAGE |
| | | | | |

	DATE		DESCRIPTION	POST. REF.	DEBIT	CREDIT	
1							1
2							2
3							3
4							4

b.

EXERCISE 19-13

a. through d.

JOURNAL

	DATE		DESCRIPTION	POST. REF.	DEBIT	CREDIT	
1							1
2							2
3							3
4							4
5							5
6							6
7							7
8							8
9							9
10							10
11							11
12							12
13							13
14							14
15							15
16							16
17							17
18							18
19							19
20							20
21							21
22							22
23							23
24							24

EXERCISE 19-14

a.

Income Statement		

b. Materials inventory:

Work in process inventory:

Finished goods inventory:

EXERCISE 19-15

a.

Date	Job No.	Quantity	Product	Amount	Unit Cost
Jan. 2	1	520	TT	$16,120	_____
Jan. 15	22	1,610	SS	20,125	_____
Feb. 3	30	1,420	SS	25,560	_____
Mar. 7	41	670	TT	15,075	_____
Mar. 24	49	2,210	SLK	22,100	_____
May 19	58	2,550	SLK	31,875	_____
June 12	65	620	TT	10,540	_____
Aug. 18	78	3,110	SLK	48,205	_____
Sept. 2	82	1,210	SS	16,940	_____
Nov. 14	92	750	TT	8,250	_____
Dec. 12	98	2,700	SLK	52,650	_____

Unit Costs for TT

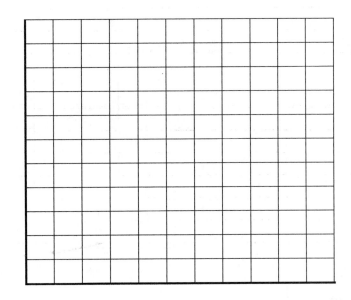

Unit Cost

Job Number

EXERCISE 19-15, Continued

Unit Costs for SS

Unit Cost

Job Number

Unit Costs for SLK

Unit Cost

Job Number

_____

_____

_____

_____

EXERCISE 19-15, Concluded

b. _____

_____

_____

_____

_____

_____

_____

_____

_____

_____

EXERCISE 19-16

a. _____

_____

_____

_____

_____

_____

_____

_____

Job 101:

EXERCISE 19-16, Continued

Job 105:

EXERCISE 19-16, Concluded

b. _____

EXERCISE 19-18

a. through d.

JOURNAL   PAGE

	DATE		DESCRIPTION	POST. REF.	DEBIT	CREDIT	
1							1
2							2
3							3
4							4
5							5
6							6
7							7
8							8
9							9
10							10
11							11
12							12

Supporting calculations:

This Page Not Used.

PROBLEM 19-2 ___

1. a. through g.

JOURNAL

	DATE		DESCRIPTION	POST. REF.	DEBIT	CREDIT	
1							1
2							2
3							3
4							4
5							5
6							6
7							7
8							8
9							9
10							10
11							11
12							12
13							13
14							14
15							15
16							16
17							17
18							18
19							19
20							20
21							21
22							22
23							23
24							24
25							25
26							26
27							27
28							28
29							29
30							30

PROBLEM 19-2 ___, Continued

   f. Computation of cost of jobs finished:

   g. Computation of cost of jobs sold:

2.

Work in Process

Finished Goods

PROBLEM 19-2 ___ , Concluded

3.

Schedule of Unfinished Jobs

JOB	DIRECT MATERIALS	DIRECT LABOR	FACTORY OVERHEAD	TOTAL

4.

Schedule of Completed Jobs

JOB	DIRECT MATERIALS	DIRECT LABOR	FACTORY OVERHEAD	TOTAL

This Page Not Used.

PROBLEM 19-3 ___

1. and 2.

JOB ORDER COST SHEET

Customer _____   Date   _____

Address   _____   Date wanted   _____

         _____   Date completed _____

Item   _____   Job No.   _____

ESTIMATE

Direct Materials	Amount	Direct Labor	Amount	Summary	Amount
___ meters at $ _____	_____	___ hours at $ _____	_____	Direct materials	_____
___ meters at _____	_____	___ hours at _____	_____	Direct labor	_____
___ meters at _____	_____	___ hours at _____	_____	Factory overhead	_____
___ meters at _____	_____	___ hours at _____	_____		
Total	_____	Total	_____	Total cost	_____

ACTUAL

	Direct Materials			Direct Labor		Summary	
Mat. Req. No.	Description	Amount	Time Ticket No.	Description	Amount	Item	Amount
____	_____	_____	____	_____	_____	Direct materials	_____
____	_____	_____	____	_____	_____	Direct labor	_____
____	_____	_____	____	_____	_____	Factory overhead	_____
____	_____	_____	____	_____	_____		
Total		_____	Total		_____	Total cost	_____

Comments:

This Page Not Used.

Chapter 19

PROBLEM 19-4 _____

1. Supporting calculations:

Job No.	Quantity	Work in Process	Direct Materials	Direct Labor	Factory Overhead	Total Cost	Unit Cost	Units Sold	Cost of Goods Sold

(A) _____

(B) _____

(C) _____

(D) _____

(E) _____

(F) _____

(G) _____

(H) _____

PROBLEM 19-4 ___, Concluded

2. _____

_____

_____

_____

_____

_____

_____

_____

_____

_____

_____

_____

_____

PROBLEM 19-5 ___

1.

Income Statement			

Supporting calculations:

_____
_____
_____
_____
_____
_____
_____
_____

PROBLEM 19-5 ___ , Concluded

2. _____

_____

_____

_____

_____

_____

_____

_____

_____

_____

_____

_____

EXERCISE 20-1

a. through e.

JOURNAL   PAGE

	DATE		DESCRIPTION	POST. REF.	DEBIT	CREDIT		
1							1	
2							2	
3							3	
4							4	
5							5	
6							6	
7							7	
8							8	
9							9	
10							10	
11							11	
12							12	
13							13	
14							14	
15							15	
16							16	
17							17	
18							18	
19							19	
20							20	
21							21	
22							22	
23							23	
24							24	
25							25	

Chapter 20

EXERCISE 20-2

EXERCISE 20-10

a.

b.

c.

EXERCISE 20-11

a.

b.

A	B	C	D
		Equivalent Units	
	Whole Units	Direct Materials	Conversion

c.

A	B	C
	Costs	
	Direct Materials	Conversion

d. _____

EXERCISE 20-12

a. **1.** _____

2. _____

3. _____

4. _____

b. _____
_____
_____
_____
_____
_____
_____

EXERCISE 20-12, Concluded

c. _____

_____

EXERCISE 20-13

EXERCISE 20-14

a. _____

b.

	A	Whole Units	Equivalent Units	
			Direct Materials	Conversion
1				
2				
3				
4				
5				
6				
7				
8				
9				
10				
11				
12				

	A	Costs	
		Direct Materials	Conversion
1			
2			
3			
4			
5			
6			
7			

c. _____

EXERCISE 20-15

a. _____

b. _____

c. _____

d. _____

e. _____

EXERCISE 20-16

a. 1. through 3.

	A	B	C	D
1				
2	Cost of Production Report—_____			
3				
4			Equivalent Units	
5	Units	Whole Units	Direct Materials	Conversion
6				
7				
8				
9				
10				
11				
12				
13				
14				
15				
16				
17				
18				
19				
20				
21				
22				
23				
24				
25				
26				
27				
28				
29				
30				

EXERCISE 20-16, Concluded

	A	B	C	D
1		Costs		
2	Costs	Direct Materials	Conversion	Total
3				
4				
5				
6				
7				
8				
9				
10				
11				
12				
13				
14				
15				
16				
17				
18				
19				
20				
21				
22				
23				
24				
25				
26				
27				
28				

b.

EXERCISE 20-17

a.

	A	B	C	D
1				
2	Cost of Production Report—_____			
3				
4			**Equivalent Units**	
5	**Units**	**Whole Units**	**Direct Materials**	**Conversion**
6				
7				
8				
9				
10				
11				
12				
13				
14				
15				
16				
17				
18				
19				
20				
21				
22				
23				
24				
25				
26				
27				
28				
29				
30				

EXERCISE 20-17, Concluded

	A	B	C	D
			Costs	
	Costs	Direct Materials	Conversion	Total
1				
2				
3				
4				
5				
6				
7				
8				
9				
10				
11				
12				
13				
14				
15				
16				
17				
18				
19				
20				
21				
22				
23				
24				
25				
26				
27				
28				

b.

EXERCISE 20-18

a. 1. through 3.

JOURNAL

	DATE		DESCRIPTION	POST. REF.	DEBIT	CREDIT	
1							1
2							2
3							3
4							4
5							5
6							6
7							7
8							8
9							9
10							10
11							11
12							12
13							13

EXERCISE 20-18, Continued

Supporting calculations:

	A	B	C	D
1			Equivalent Units	
2		Whole Units	Direct Materials	Conversion
3				
4				
5				
6				
7				
8				
9				
10				

EXERCISE 20-18, Concluded

b. _____

c.

EXERCISE 20-19

a. 1. through 3.

JOURNAL   PAGE

	DATE		DESCRIPTION	POST. REF.	DEBIT	CREDIT	
1							1
2							2
3							3
4							4
5							5
6							6
7							7
8							8
9							9
10							10
11							11
12							12
13							13

EXERCISE 20-19, Concluded

Supporting calculations:

	A	B	C	D
1			**Equivalent Units**	
2		**Whole Units**	**Direct Materials**	**Conversion**
3				
4				
5				
6				
7				
8				
9				
10				

b.

EXERCISE 20-20

_____

_____

_____

_____

_____

	A	B	C	D	E
1					
2					
3					
4					

_____

_____

_____

_____

_____

_____

_____

	A	B	C	D	E
1					
2					
3					
4					
5					
6					
7					
8					
9					
10					

EXERCISE 20-20, Concluded

EXERCISE 20-21

a.

	A	B	C	D	E	F	G
1		January	February	March	April	May	June
2							
3							
4							
5							

_____

_____

_____

_____

_____

EXERCISE 20-21, Concluded

b. _____

EXERCISE 20-22

EXERCISE 20-22, Concluded

APPENDIX EXERCISE 20-23

a. and b.

	A	B	C
1		a. Whole Units	b. Equivalent Units of Production
2			
3			
4			
5			
6			
7			
8			
9			
10			
11			
12			

APPENDIX EXERCISE 20-24

a. Drawing Department

	A	B	C
1		Whole Units	Equivalent Units of Production
2			
3			
4			
5			
6			
7			
8			
9			
10			
11			
12			

APPENDIX EXERCISE 20-24, Concluded

b. Winding Department

A	B	C
1	**Whole Units**	**Equivalent Units of Production**
2		
3		
4		
5		
6		
7		
8		
9		
10		
11		
12		

APPENDIX EXERCISE 20-25

a.

b.

A	B	C
1	**Whole Units**	**Equivalent Units of Production**
2		
3		
4		
5		
6		
7		
8		
9		
10		
11		
12		

APPENDIX EXERCISE 20-26

a. and b.

	A	B	C
1		**Whole Units**	**Equivalent Units of Production**
2			
3			
4			
5			
6			
7			
8			
9			
10			
11			
12			

c. _____

_____

_____

_____

_____

d. _____

_____

e. _____

_____

APPENDIX EXERCISE 20-27

a.

	A	Whole Units	Equivalent Units of Production
1			
2			
3			
4			
5			
6			
7			
8			
9			
10			
11			
12			

_____

_____

_____

_____

_____

b. _____

_____

c. _____

_____

APPENDIX EXERCISE 20-28

	A	B	C
1			
2	Cost of Production Report—Roasting Department		
3			
4	Units	Whole Units	Equivalent Units of Production
5			
6			
7			
8			
9			
10			
11			
12			
13			
14			
15			
16			

	A	B
1	Costs	
2		
3		
4		
5		
6		
7		
8		
9		
10		
11		
12		
13		
14		
15		
16		
17		
18		
19		
20		

APPENDIX EXERCISE 20-29

	A	B	C
1			
2	**Cost of Production Report—Cutting Department**		
3			
4	**Units**	**Whole Units**	**Equivalent Units of Production**
5			
6			
7			
8			
9			
10			
11			
12			
13			
14			
15			
16			

	A	B
1	**Costs**	
2		
3		
4		
5		
6		
7		
8		
9		
10		
11		
12		
13		
14		
15		
16		
17		
18		
19		
20		

PROBLEM 20-1 ___

1. a. through i.

JOURNAL

	DATE		DESCRIPTION	POST. REF.	DEBIT	CREDIT	
1							1
2							2
3							3
4							4
5							5
6							6
7							7
8							8
9							9
10							10
11							11
12							12
13							13
14							14
15							15
16							16
17							17
18							18
19							19
20							20
21							21
22							22
23							23
24							24
25							25
26							26
27							27
28							28
29							29
30							30
31							31
32							32
33							33
34							34
35							35

PROBLEM 20-1 ___, Continued

JOURNAL   PAGE ___

	DATE		DESCRIPTION	POST. REF.	DEBIT	CREDIT	
1							1
2							2
3							3
4							4
5							5
6							6
7							7
8							8
9							9
10							10
11							11
12							12
13							13
14							14
15							15
16							16
17							17
18							18
19							19
20							20
21							21
22							22
23							23
24							24
25							25
26							26
27							27
28							28
29							29
30							30
31							31
32							32
33							33
34							34
35							35
36							36

PROBLEM 20-1 ___, Concluded

2.

	MATERIALS	WORK IN PROCESS— _____ DEPT.	WORK IN PROCESS— _____ DEPT.	FINISHED GOODS

3.

	FACTORY OVERHEAD— _____ DEPT.	FACTORY OVERHEAD— _____ DEPT.

This Page Not Used.

PROBLEM 20-3 ___

1.

	A	B	C	D
1				
2	**Cost of Production Report—_____**			
3				
4		**Whole Units**	**Equivalent Units**	
5			**Direct Materials**	**Conversion**
6				
7				
8				
9				
10				
11				
12				
13				
14				
15				
16				
17				
18				
19				
20				
21				
22				
23				
24				
25				
26				
27				
28				
29				
30				
31				
32				
33				
34				
35				
36				
37				
38				
39				
40				
41				
42				

PROBLEM 20-3 ___, Continued

	A	B	C	D
	Costs	Costs		
		Direct Materials	Conversion	Total
3				
4				
5				
6				
7				
8				
9				
10				
11				
12				
13				
14				
15				
16				
17				
18				
19				
20				
21				
22				
23				
24				
25				
26				
27				
28				
29				
30				
31				
32				
33				
34				
35				
36				
37				
38				
39				

PROBLEM 20-3 ___, Concluded

2.

JOURNAL   PAGE

	DATE		DESCRIPTION	POST. REF.	DEBIT	CREDIT	
1							1
2							2
3							3
4							4
5							5
6							6
7							7
8							8
9							9
10							10

3. _____

_____

4. _____

_____

_____

_____

_____

_____

_____

_____

_____

_____

This Page Not Used.

APPENDIX PROBLEM 20-5 ___

	A	B	C
1			
2	Cost of Production Report—_____		
3			
4	Units	Whole Units	Equivalent Units of Production
5			
6			
7			
8			
9			
10			
11			
12			
13			
14			
15			
16			
17			
18			
19			
20			

	A	B
1	Costs	
2		
3		
4		
5		
6		
7		
8		
9		
10		
11		
12		
13		
14		
15		
16		
17		
18		
19		
20		

This Page Not Used.

EXERCISE 21-1

1. _____
2. _____
3. _____
4. _____
5. _____
6. _____
7. _____
8. _____

9. _____
10. _____
11. _____
12. _____
13. _____
14. _____
15. _____

EXERCISE 21-2

a. _____
b. _____
c. _____

d. _____
e. _____

EXERCISE 21-3

1. Financial aid office salaries: _____
2. Office supplies: _____
3. Instructor salaries: _____
4. Housing personnel wages: _____
5. Student records office salaries: _____
6. Admissions office salaries: _____

EXERCISE 21-4

1. Preparation costs for each car received: _____
2. Salespersons' commission of 5% of the sales price for each car sold: _____
3. Administrative costs for ordering cars: _____

EXERCISE 21-5

a. _____
b. _____
c. _____
d. _____
e. _____
f. _____

g. _____
h. _____
i. _____
j. _____
k. _____

EXERCISE 21-6

Components produced...............	400,000		480,000		600,000
Total costs:					
Total variable costs...............	$160,000	**(d)** _____		**(j)** _____	
Total fixed costs....................	24,000	**(e)** _____		**(k)** _____	
Total costs	$400,000	**(f)** _____		**(l)** _____	
Cost per unit:					
Variable cost per unit............	**(a)** _____	**(g)** _____		**(m)** _____	
Fixed cost per unit	**(b)** _____	**(h)** _____		**(n)** _____	
Total cost per unit	**(c)** _____	**(i)** _____		**(o)** _____	

Supporting calculations:

_____

_____

_____

_____

_____

_____

_____

_____

_____

_____

_____

_____

_____

_____

_____

_____

_____

_____

_____

_____

_____

EXERCISE 21-7

a. Variable cost per unit: _____

_____

_____

_____

_____

_____

_____

_____

Fixed cost: _____

_____

_____

_____

_____

_____

_____

_____

_____

_____

_____

_____

_____

_____

b. _____

_____

_____

EXERCISE 21-8

Variable Cost per Gross-Ton Mile: _____

_____

_____

_____

_____

_____

_____

_____

Fixed Cost: _____

_____

_____

_____

_____

_____

_____

_____

_____

_____

_____

_____

_____

_____

_____

EXERCISE 21-9

a.

b.

EXERCISE 21-10

a.

b.

EXERCISE 21-10, Concluded

c.

EXERCISE 21-11

a. _____

_____

_____

_____

_____

b. _____

_____

_____

_____

_____

EXERCISE 21-12

a. _____

_____

_____

_____

_____

_____

_____

_____

_____

_____

_____

EXERCISE 21-12, Concluded

b. _____

_____

_____

_____

_____

EXERCISE 21-13

a. _____

_____

_____

_____

_____

b. _____

_____

_____

_____

_____

EXERCISE 21-14

EXERCISE 21-15

EXERCISE 21-16

a. _____

_____

_____

_____

_____

_____

_____

_____

_____

b. _____

_____

_____

_____

_____

_____

_____

_____

_____

_____

_____

_____

EXERCISE 21-17

a.

Sales and Costs

Units of Sales

b. _____

_____

c. _____

_____

_____

_____

_____

EXERCISE 21-18

a. _____
   _____

b.

c.

Operating Profit (Loss)

Units of Sales

d. _____
   _____

EXERCISE 21-19

Chart name: _____

a. _____

b. _____

c. _____

d. _____

e. _____

f. _____

EXERCISE 21-20

Chart name: _____

a. _____

b. _____

c. _____

d. _____

e. _____

f. _____

EXERCISE 21-21

a. _____

_____

_____

_____

_____

_____

_____

_____

_____

_____

_____

_____

_____

_____

b. Baseball bats: _____

_____

Baseball gloves: _____

_____

EXERCISE 21-22

a. _____

_____

_____

_____

_____

_____

_____

Supporting calculations:

b.

EXERCISE 21-23

a. (1) In dollars: _____

_____

_____

_____

_____

(2) As a percentage of sales: _____

_____

_____

_____

_____

b. _____

_____

_____

_____

_____

_____

_____

_____

_____

_____

_____

_____

_____

_____

_____

_____

_____

_____

_____

_____

EXERCISE 21-24

_____

_____

_____

_____

EXERCISE 21-25

a. Beck Inc. operating leverage: _____

_____

_____

_____

_____

_____

Bryant Inc. operating leverage: _____

_____

_____

_____

_____

_____

_____

b. _____

_____

_____

_____

_____

c. _____

_____

_____

_____

_____

_____

APPENDIX EXERCISE 21-26

a. _____

b. _____

c. _____

APPENDIX EXERCISE 21-27

a.

	Income Statement—Variable Costing		

Computations:

APPENDIX EXERCISE 21-27, Concluded

b.

APPENDIX EXERCISE 21-28

a.

Income Statement—Absorption Costing		

Computations:

APPENDIX EXERCISE 21-28, Concluded

b.

This Page Not Used.

PROBLEM 21-1 ___

Cost	Fixed Cost	Variable Cost	Mixed Cost
a.			
b.			
c.			
d.			
e.			
f.			
g.			
h.			
i.			
j.			
k.			
l.			
m.			
n.			
o.			
p.			
q.			
r.			
s.			
t.			

This Page Not Used.

PROBLEM 21-2 ___

1.

2. a. Unit variable cost: _____

_____

  b. Unit contribution margin: _____

_____

3. _____

_____

_____

_____

_____

_____

_____

PROBLEM 21-2 ___, Continued

4. _____

5. _____

6.

7.

PROBLEM 21-2 ___ , Concluded

8. _____

_____

_____

_____

_____

_____

_____

_____

_____

_____

_____

_____

_____

_____

_____

_____

_____

_____

_____

_____

_____

_____

This Page Not Used.

PROBLEM 21-3 ___

1. Break-even sales (units): _____

_____

_____

_____

_____

_____

_____

_____

_____

_____

_____

2. Sales (units): _____

_____

_____

_____

_____

_____

_____

_____

_____

_____

_____

_____

_____

PROBLEM 21-3 ___, Concluded

3.

Sales and Costs

Units of Sales

4.

PROBLEM 21-4 ___

1.

Sales and Costs

Units of Sales

PROBLEM 21-4 ___, Continued

PROBLEM 21-4 ___, Continued

2.

Sales and Costs

Units of Sales

PROBLEM 21-4 ___, Continued

3.

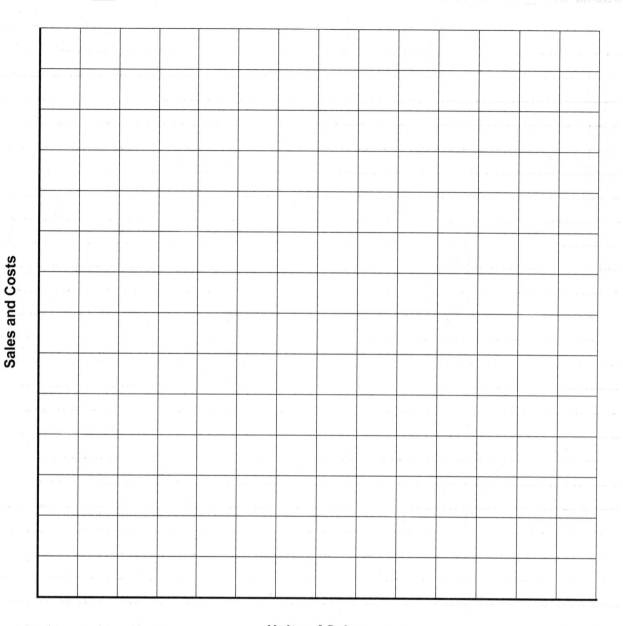

Sales and Costs

Units of Sales

PROBLEM 21-4 ___ , Continued

PROBLEM 21-4 ___ , Concluded

4.

Sales and Costs

Units of Sales

PROBLEM 21-5 ___

1.

2.

PROBLEM 21-5 ___ , Concluded

3.

PROBLEM 21-6 ___

1.

Estimated Income Statement			

PROBLEM 21-6 ___, Continued

2. _____

_____

_____

_____

_____

_____

_____

_____

_____

_____

_____

3. _____

_____

_____

_____

_____

_____

_____

_____

_____

_____

_____

_____

_____

_____

_____

_____

_____

_____

PROBLEM 21-6 ___, Continued

4.

Sales and Costs

Units

PROBLEM 21-6 ___, Concluded

5.

6.

EXERCISE 22-1

a.

	A	B	C	D	E
1		JEN LASSITER			
2		Cash Budget			
3		For the Four Months Ending December 31, 2014			
4		September	October	November	December
5					
6					
7					
8					
9					
10					
11					
12					
13					
14					
15					
16					
17					
18					
19					
20					
21					
22					
23					
24					

b. _____

_____

_____

EXERCISE 22-1, Concluded

c. _____

_____

_____

_____

_____

_____

_____

_____

_____

_____

_____

_____

_____

_____

_____

_____

_____

_____

_____

_____

_____

_____

_____

EXERCISE 22-2

	A	B	C	D
1	CYBERWARE			
2	Flexible Selling and Administrative Expenses Budget			
3	For the Month Ending March 31, 2014			
4				
5				
6				
7				
8				
9				
10				
11				
12				
13				
14				
15				
16				
17				
18				
19				
20				
21				
22				
23				
24				
25				

EXERCISE 22-3

a.

	A	B	C	D
1	GILMAN COMPANY—MACHINING DEPARTMENT			
2	Flexible Production Budget			
3	For the Three Months Ending March 31, 2014			
4		January	February	March
5				
6				
7				
8				
9				
10				
11				
12				
13				
14				
15				
16				
17				
18				
19				
20				
21				
22				

_____

_____

_____

_____

EXERCISE 22-3, Concluded

b.

	JANUARY	FEBRUARY	MARCH

_____

_____

_____

_____

_____

_____

_____

_____

_____

_____

EXERCISE 22-4

	A	B	C	D
1	STEELCASE INC.—FABRICATION DEPARTMENT			
2	Flexible Production Budget			
3	August 2014			
4	(assumed data)			
5				
6				
7				
8				
9				
10				
11				
12				
13				
14				
15				
16				
17				
18				

EXERCISE 22-5

	A	B	C
1	ACCUWEIGHT INC.		
2	Production Budget		
3	For the Month Ended July 31, 2015		
4		Units	
5		Small Scale	Large Scale
6			
7			
8			
9			
10			
11			
12			
13			

EXERCISE 22-6

a.

	A	B	C	D
1	SOUNDLAB INC.			
2	Sales Budget			
3	For the Three Months Ending November 30, 2014			
4	Product and Area	Unit Sales Volume	Unit Selling Price	Total Sales
5				
6				
7				
8				
9				
10				
11				
12				
13				
14				

EXERCISE 22-6, Concluded

b.

	A	B	C
1	SOUNDLAB INC.		
2	Production Budget		
3	For the Month Ended November 30, 2014		
4		Units	
5		Model DL	Model XL
6			
7			
8			
9			
10			
11			
12			
13			

EXERCISE 22-7

	A	B	C	D
1	ROLLINS AND COHEN, CPAs			
2	Professional Fees Earned Budget			
3	For the Year Ending December 31, 2014			
4		Billable Hours	Hourly Rate	Total Revenue
5				
6				
7				
8				
9				
10				
11				
12				
13				
14				
15				
16				
17				
18				
19				

EXERCISE 22-8

	A	B	C
1	ROLLINS AND COHEN, CPAs		
2	Professional Labor Cost Budget		
3	For the Year Ending December 31, 2014		
4		Staff	Partners
5			
6			
7			
8			
9			
10			
11			
12			

EXERCISE 22-9

	A	B	C	D	E
1	MORETTI'S FROZEN PIZZA INC.				
2	Direct Materials Purchases Budget				
3	For the Month Ending September 30, 2014				
4		Dough	Tomato	Cheese	Total
5					
6					
7					
8					
9					
10					
11					
12					
13					
14					
15					
16					
17					
18					
19					
20					

EXERCISE 22-10

	A	B	C	D
1	COCA-COLA ENTERPRISES—WAKEFIELD PLANT			
2	Direct Materials Purchases Budget			
3	For the Month Ending May 31, 2014			
4	(assumed data)			
5		Concentrate	2-Liter Bottles	Carbonated Water
6				
7				
8				
9				
10				
11				
12				
13				
14				
15				

EXERCISE 22-11

	A	B	C	D
1	SAFETY GRIP COMPANY			
2	Direct Materials Purchases Budget			
3	For the Year Ending December 31, 2014			
4		Rubber	Steel Belts	Total
5				
6				
7				
8				
9				
10				
11				
12				
13				
14				
15				
16				
17				
18				
19				

EXERCISE 22-12

	A	B	C
1	ACE RACKET COMPANY		
2	Direct Labor Cost Budget		
3	For the Year Ending July 31, 2014		
4		Forming Department	Assembly Department
5			
6			
7			
8			
9			
10			
11			
12			

EXERCISE 22-13

	A	B	C
1	**AMBASSADOR SUITES INC.**		
2	**Direct Labor Cost Budget**		
3	**For a Weekday or a Weekend Day**		
4		**Weekday**	**Weekend Day**
5			
6			
7			
8			
9			
10			
11			
12			
13			
14			
15			
16			
17			
18			
19			
20			
21			
22			
23			
24			
25			
26			
27			
28			
29			
30			

EXERCISE 22-14

a.

	A	B	C
1	LEVI STRAUSS & CO.		
2	Production Budget		
3	May 2014		
4	(assumed data)		
5		Dockers®	501 Jeans®
6			
7			
8			
9			
10			
11			
12			
13			
14			

b.

	A	B	C	D	E	F
1	LEVI STRAUSS & CO.					
2	Direct Labor Cost Budget					
3	May 2014					
4	(assumed data)					
5		Inseam	Outerseam	Pockets	Zipper	Total
6						
7						
8						
9						
10						
11						
12						
13						
14						
15						

EXERCISE 22-15

	A	B	C
1	**SWEET TOOTH CANDY COMPANY**		
2	**Factory Overhead Cost Budget**		
3	**For the Month Ending August 31, 2014**		
4			
5			
6			
7			
8			
9			
10			
11			
12			
13			
14			
15			
16			
17			
18			

EXERCISE 22-16

	A	B	C	D
1	DELAWARE CHEMICAL COMPANY			
2	Cost of Goods Sold Budget			
3	For the Month Ending June 30, 2015			
4				
5				
6				
7				
8				
9				
10				
11				
12				
13				
14				
15				
16				
17				
18				
19				
20				
21				
22				
23				
24				
25				
26				
27				
28				
29				
30				
31				
32				

EXERCISE 22-17

	A	B	C	D
1	MINGWARE CERAMICS INC.			
2	Cost of Goods Sold Budget			
3	For the Month Ending September 30, 2014			
4				
5				
6				
7				
8				
9				
10				
11				
12				
13				
14				
15				
16				
17				
18				
19				
20				
21				
22				
23				
24				
25				
26				
27				
28				
29				
30				
31				
32				
33				

EXERCISE 22-18

	A	B	C	D
1	PETCARE SUPPLIES INC.			
2	Schedule of Collections from Sales			
3	For the Three Months Ending July 31, 2014			
4		May	June	July
5				
6				
7				
8				
9				
10				
11				
12				
13				
14				
15				
16				
17				
18				
19				
20				
21				
22				
23				
24				
25				
26				
27				

EXERCISE 22-19

	A	B	C	D
1		OFFICEMART INC.		
2		Schedule of Collections from Sales		
3		For the Three Months Ending December 31, 2014		
4		October	November	December
5				
6				
7				
8				
9				
10				
11				
12				
13				
14				
15				
16				
17				
18				
19				
20				
21				
22				
23				
24				
25				
26				
27				
28				
29				
30				

EXERCISE 22-20

	A	B	C	D
1	GREEN MOUNTAIN FINANCIAL INC.			
2	Schedule of Cash Payments for Selling and Administrative Expenses			
3	For the Three Months Ending May 31, 2014			
4		March	April	May
5				
6				
7				
8				
9				
10				
11				
12				
13				
14				
15				
16				
17				
18				
19				

EXERCISE 22-21

	A	B	C	D
1	EASTGATE PHYSICAL THERAPY INC.			
2	Schedule of Cash Payments for Operations			
3	For the Three Months Ending March 31, 2015			
4		January	February	March
5				
6				
7				
8				
9				
10				

EXERCISE 22-22

	A	B	C	D	E
1	OMICRON INC.				
2	Capital Expenditures Budget				
3	For the Four Years Ending December 31, 2014–2017				
4		2014	2015	2016	2017
5					
6					
7					
8					
9					
10					

PROBLEM 22-1 ___

1.

	UNIT SALES, YEAR ENDED 2014		INCREASE (DECREASE) ACTUAL OVER BUDGET	
	BUDGET	ACTUAL SALES	AMOUNT	PERCENT

2.

	2014 ACTUAL UNITS	PERCENTAGE INCREASE (DECREASE)	2015 BUDGETED UNITS (ROUNDED)

PROBLEM 22-1 ___, Concluded

3.

	A	B	C	D
		Sales Budget		
1				
2				
3				
4	**Product and Area**	**Unit Sales Volume**	**Unit Selling Price**	**Total Sales**
5				
6				
7				
8				
9				
10				
11				
12				
13				
14				
15				
16				

PROBLEM 22-2 ___

1.

	A	B	C	D
1				
2	Sales Budget			
3				
4	Product and Area	Unit Sales Volume	Unit Selling Price	Total Sales
5				
6				
7				
8				
9				
10				
11				
12				
13				
14				
15				
16				

2.

	A	B	C
1			
2	Production Budget		
3			
4		Units	
5			
6			
7			
8			
9			
10			
11			
12			
13			

PROBLEM 22-2 ___ , Concluded

3.

	A	B	C	D	E	F
1						
2		**Direct Materials Purchases Budget**				
3						
4						
5						
6						
7						
8						
9						
10						
11						
12						
13						
14						
15						
16						
17						
18						
19						
20						

4.

	A	B	C	D	E
1					
2		**Direct Labor Cost Budget**			
3					
4		Department	Department	Department	Total
5					
6					
7					
8					
9					
10					
11					
12					
13					
14					

PROBLEM 22-3 ___

1.

	A	B	C	D
1				
2	Sales Budget			
3				
4		Unit Sales Volume	Unit Selling Price	Total Sales
5				
6				
7				
8				

2.

	A	B	C
1			
2	Production Budget		
3			
4		Units	
5			
6			
7			
8			
9			
10			
11			
12			
13			

PROBLEM 22-3 ___, Continued

3.

	A	B	C	D
1				
2	**Direct Materials Purchases Budget**			
3				
4				**Total**
5				
6				
7				
8				
9				
10				
11				
12				
13				
14				
15				
16				
17				
18				
19				
20				

PROBLEM 22-3 ___, Continued

4.

	A	B	C	D
1				
2	**Direct Labor Cost Budget**			
3				
4		**Department**	**Department**	**Total**
5				
6				
7				
8				
9				
10				
11				
12				

5.

	A	B
1		
2	**Factory Overhead Cost Budget**	
3		
4		
5		
6		
7		
8		
9		
10		

PROBLEM 22-3 ___, Continued

6.

	A	B	C	D
1				
2	**Cost of Goods Sold Budget**			
3				
4				
5				
6				
7				
8				
9				
10				
11				
12				
13				
14				
15				
16				
17				
18				
19				
20				
21				
22				
23				
24				
25				
26				
27				
28				
29				
30				
31				
32				
33				
34				

PROBLEM 22-3 ___, Continued

7.

	A	B	C
1			
2	**Selling and Administrative Expenses Budget**		
3			
4			
5			
6			
7			
8			
9			
10			
11			
12			
13			
14			
15			
16			
17			
18			
19			
20			
21			
22			
23			
24			

PROBLEM 22-3 ___, Concluded

8.

	A	B	C
1			
2	**Budgeted Income Statement**		
3			
4			
5			
6			
7			
8			
9			
10			
11			
12			
13			
14			
15			
16			
17			
18			
19			
20			

PROBLEM 22-4 ___

1.

	A	B	C	D
1				
2	Cash Budget			
3				
4				
5				
6				
7				
8				
9				
10				
11				
12				
13				
14				
15				
16				
17				
18				
19				
20				
21				
22				
23				
24				
25				
26				
27				
28				
29				
30				

PROBLEM 22-4 ___, Continued

Computations:

PROBLEM 22-4 ___, Concluded

2. _____

_____

_____

_____

_____

_____

_____

_____

_____

_____

This Page Not Used.

PROBLEM 22-5 ___

1.

	A	B	C	D
1				
2	**Budgeted Income Statement**			
3				
4				
5				
6				
7				
8				
9				
10				
11				
12				
13				
14				
15				
16				
17				
18				
19				
20				
21				
22				
23				
24				
25				
26				
27				
28				
29				
30				
31				
32				
33				
34				

PROBLEM 22-5 ___, Continued

2.

	A	B	C	D
1				
2	Budgeted Balance Sheet			
3				
4				
5				
6				
7				
8				
9				
10				
11				
12				
13				
14				
15				
16				
17				
18				
19				
20				
21				
22				
23				
24				
25				
26				

PROBLEM 22-5 ___, Concluded

Supporting calculations:

This Page Not Used.

EXERCISE 23-1

Ingredient	Quantity	x	Price	Total
		x		
		x		
		x		

_____
_____
_____
_____
_____

EXERCISE 23-2

a.

b. _____
_____
_____
_____
_____
_____
_____
_____

EXERCISE 23-3

a.

	A	B
1	TIME IN A BOTTLE COMPANY	
2	Manufacturing Cost Budget	
3	For the Month Ended May 31, 2014	
4		Standard Cost at Planned Volume (600,000 Bottles)
5		
6		
7		
8		
9		
10		
11		
12		
13		
14		
15		
16		

b.

	A	B	C	D
1	TIME IN A BOTTLE COMPANY			
2	Manufacturing Costs—Budget Performance Report			
3	For the Month Ended May 31, 2014			
4		Actual Costs	Standard Costs at Actual Volume (610,000 Bottles)	Cost Variance— (Favorable) Unfavorable
5				
6				
7				
8				
9				
10				
11				
12				
13				
14				
15				
16				
17				

EXERCISE 23-3, Concluded

c. _____

_____

_____

_____

_____

EXERCISE 23-4

a. Price variance: _____

_____

_____

_____

_____

_____

_____

Quantity variance: _____

_____

_____

_____

_____

_____

_____

Total direct materials cost variance: _____

_____

_____

_____

_____

_____

EXERCISE 23-4, Concluded

b. _____

_____

_____

_____

_____

_____

_____

_____

_____

_____

_____

_____

_____

_____

_____

_____

_____

_____

_____

_____

_____

_____

_____

EXERCISE 23-5

Price variance: _____

_____

_____

_____

_____

_____

_____

Quantity variance: _____

_____

_____

_____

_____

_____

Total direct materials cost variance: _____

_____

_____

_____

_____

_____

EXERCISE 23-6

Alternate solution:

Proof:

_____

_____

_____

_____

_____

_____

_____

_____

_____

_____

EXERCISE 23-7

a.

b.

EXERCISE 23-8

a. Rate variance: _____

_____

_____

_____

_____

_____

_____

Time variance: _____

_____

_____

_____

_____

_____

_____

Total direct labor cost variance: _____

_____

_____

_____

_____

_____

_____

b. _____

_____

_____

_____

_____

_____

_____

_____

EXERCISE 23-9

a. Rate variance: _____

_____

_____

_____

_____

_____

_____

Time variance: _____

_____

_____

_____

_____

_____

_____

_____

Total direct labor cost variance: _____

_____

_____

_____

_____

_____

_____

b. Debit to Work in Process: _____

EXERCISE 23-10

a. (1) Cutting Department

Rate variance: _____

_____

_____

_____

_____

_____

_____

Time variance: _____

_____

_____

_____

_____

_____

_____

Total direct labor cost variance: _____

_____

_____

_____

_____

_____

_____

EXERCISE 23-10, Continued

(2) Sewing Department

Rate variance: _____

_____

_____

_____

_____

_____

_____

Time variance: _____

_____

_____

_____

_____

_____

_____

Total direct labor cost variance: _____

_____

_____

_____

_____

_____

_____

EXERCISE 23-10, Concluded

b. _____

_____

_____

_____

_____

_____

_____

_____

_____

_____

_____

_____

_____

_____

EXERCISE 23-11

a. _____

_____

b.

c.

EXERCISE 23-12

a. _____

b. _____

EXERCISE 23-13

Step 1: _____

_____

_____

_____

_____

_____

_____

_____

_____

_____

_____

_____

_____

_____

_____

_____

_____

_____

_____

_____

_____

_____

_____

Step 2: _____

_____

_____

EXERCISE 23-13, Concluded

Step 3: _____

_____

_____

EXERCISE 23-14

	A	B	C	D
1	**LENO MANUFACTURING COMPANY**			
2	**Factory Overhead Cost Budget—Press Department**			
3	**For the Month Ended November 30, 2014**			
4				
5				
6				
7				
8				
9				
10				
11				
12				
13				
14				
15				
16				
17				
18				
19				
20				

EXERCISE 23-15

a.

	A	B	C	D
1	WIKI WIKI COMPANY			
2	Monthly Factory Overhead Cost Budget—Fabrication Department			
3				
4				
5				
6				
7				
8				
9				

b. Overhead applied to actual production:

EXERCISE 23-16

Variable factory overhead controllable variance:

Fixed factory overhead volume variance:

Total factory overhead cost variance:

EXERCISE 23-16, Concluded

Alternative Computation of Overhead Variances:

EXERCISE 23-17

a. Controllable variance:

b. Volume variance:

Total factory overhead cost variance:

EXERCISE 23-17, Concluded

Alternative Computation of Overhead Variances:

EXERCISE 23-18

_____
_____
_____
_____
_____
_____
_____
_____

Correct Determination of Factory Overhead Cost Variances:

EXERCISE 23-18, Concluded

Alternative Computation of Overhead Variances:

EXERCISE 23-19

	A	B	C	D	E
1	TANNIN PRODUCTS INC.				
2	Factory Overhead Cost Variance Report—Trim Department				
3	For the Month Ending July 31, 2014				
4	Productive capacity for the month				
5	Actual productive capacity used for the month				
6					
7		Budget (at actual production)	Actual	Variances	
8					
9				Favorable	Unfavorable
10					
11					
12					
13					
14					
15					
16					
17					
18					
19					
20					
21					
22					
23					
24					
25					
26					
27					
28					
29					
30					
31					
32					
33					
34					
35					
36					
37					
38					
39					
40					

EXERCISE 23-19, Concluded

Alternative Computation of Overhead Variances:

EXERCISE 23-20

a. and b.

JOURNAL   PAGE

	DATE		DESCRIPTION	POST. REF.	DEBIT	CREDIT	
1							1
2							2
3							3
4							4
5							5
6							6
7							7
8							8

EXERCISE 23-21

JOURNAL   PAGE

	DATE		DESCRIPTION	POST. REF.	DEBIT	CREDIT	
1							1
2							2
3							3
4							4
5							5

EXERCISE 23-22

	Income Statement		
	FAVORABLE	UNFAVORABLE	

EXERCISE 23-23

a. and b.

	Input Measure	Output Measure	Explanation
Average computer response time to customer "clicks"			
Dollar amount of returned goods			
Elapsed time between customer order and product delivery			
Maintenance dollars divided by hardware investment			
Number of customer complaints divided by the number of orders			
Number of misfilled orders divided by the number of orders			
Number of orders per warehouse employee			
Number of page faults or errors due to software programming errors			
Number of software fixes per week			
Server (computer) downtime			
Training dollars per programmer			

EXERCISE 23-24

a. Input Measures: _____

_____

_____

_____

_____

_____

_____

_____

Output Measures: _____

_____

_____

_____

_____

_____

_____

_____

_____

_____

_____

_____

_____

b. _____

_____

_____

_____

_____

_____

_____

_____

_____

_____

_____

This Page Not Used.

PROBLEM 23-1 ___

a.

b.   **___ls Cost Variance**

Price variance: _____

_____

_____

_____

_____

_____

_____

Quantity variance: _____

_____

_____

_____

_____

_____

_____

_____

Total direct materials cost variance: _____

_____

_____

_____

_____

_____

_____

PROBLEM 23-1 ___, Concluded

c.   <u>**Direct Labor Cost Variance**</u>

Rate variance: _____

_____

_____

_____

_____

_____

_____

Time variance: _____

_____

_____

_____

_____

_____

_____

Total direct labor cost variance: _____

_____

_____

_____

_____

_____

_____

PROBLEM 23-2 ___

1. a.

			TOTAL

PROBLEM 23-2 ___, Continued

b.

			TOTAL

PROBLEM 23-2 ___, Concluded

2. _____

_____

_____

_____

_____

_____

_____

_____

_____

_____

This Page Not Used.

PROBLEM 23-3 ___

a.   <u>**Direct Materials Cost Variance**</u>

Price variance: _____

_____

_____

_____

_____

_____

_____

Quantity variance: _____

_____

_____

_____

_____

_____

_____

Total direct materials cost variance: _____

_____

_____

_____

_____

_____

_____

PROBLEM 23-3 ___, Continued

b.   <u>**Direct Labor Cost Variance**</u>

Rate variance: _____

_____

_____

_____

_____

_____

_____

Time variance: _____

_____

_____

_____

_____

_____

_____

Total direct labor cost variance: _____

_____

_____

_____

_____

_____

_____

PROBLEM 23-3 ___, Continued

c.   <u>Factory Overhead Cost Variance</u>

PROBLEM 23-3 ___, Concluded

Alternative Computation of Overhead Variances:

PROBLEM 23-4 ___

	A	B	C	D	E
1					
2	Factory Overhead Cost Variance Report—_____ Department				
3					
4	Normal capacity for the month				
5	Actual production for the month				
6					
7				Variances	
8		Budget	Actual	Favorable	Unfavorable
9					
10					
11					
12					
13					
14					
15					
16					
17					
18					
19					
20					
21					
22					
23					
24					
25					
26					
27					
28					
29					
30					
31					
32					
33					
34					
35					
36					
37					
38					
39					
40					

PROBLEM 23-4 ___, Concluded

Alternative Computation of Overhead Variances:

PROBLEM 23-5 ___

1.

2.

3.

PROBLEM 23-5 ___, Continued

4.

5.

PROBLEM 23-5 ___, Concluded

6. _____

_____

_____

_____

_____

_____

_____

_____

_____

_____

This Page Not Used.

COMPREHENSIVE PROBLEM 5

Part A

1. _____

2.

3.

4. _____

COMPREHENSIVE PROBLEM 5, Continued

Part B

5.

Production Budget

	CASES

6.

Direct Materials Purchases Budget

	CREAM BASE (OZS.)	NATURAL OILS (OZS.)	BOTTLES (BOTTLES)	TOTAL

COMPREHENSIVE PROBLEM 5, Continued

7.

	Direct Labor Budget			
		MIXING	FILLING	TOTAL

8.

	Factory Overhead Budget			

COMPREHENSIVE PROBLEM 5, Continued

9.

Budgeted Income Statement			

COMPREHENSIVE PROBLEM 5, Continued

Part C

10. Direct Materials Price Variance:

	CREAM BASE	NATURAL OILS	BOTTLES	

_____

_____

_____

_____

_____

Direct Materials Quantity Variance:

	CREAM BASE	NATURAL OILS	BOTTLES	

_____

_____

_____

_____

_____

_____

_____

COMPREHENSIVE PROBLEM 5, Continued

11. Direct Labor Rate Variance:

	MIXING DEPARTMENT	FILLING DEPARTMENT

_____
_____
_____
_____
_____
_____
_____

Direct Labor Time Variance:

	MIXING DEPARTMENT	FILLING DEPARTMENT

_____
_____
_____
_____
_____
_____
_____
_____
_____
_____
_____

COMPREHENSIVE PROBLEM 5, Continued

12. Factory Overhead Controllable Variance:

13. Factory Overhead Volume Variance:

_____

_____

_____

COMPREHENSIVE PROBLEM 5, Continued

Alternative Computation of Overhead Variances:

COMPREHENSIVE PROBLEM 5, Concluded

14. _____

_____

_____

_____

_____

_____

_____

_____

_____

_____

_____

_____

This Page Not Used.

14 #17

EXERCISE 24-1

a.

Maguire Company
Budget Performance Report—Vice President, Production
For the Month Ended May 31, 2014

Plant	Budget	Actual	Over Budget	Under Budget
Mid-Atlantic Region	$748,800	$747,000		$1,800
West Region	~~680~~	532,800		2,880
South Region	_____	**(i)** $ _____	_____
	_____	**(l)** $ _____	$4,680

Company
—Manager, South Region Plant
nded May 31, 2014

Department	Budget	Actual	Over Budget	Under Budget
Chip Fabrication	**(a)** $ _____	**(b)** $ _____	**(c)** $ _____	
Electronic Assembly	153,216	155,232	2,016	
Final Assembly	246,600	245,952		$648
	(d) $ _____	**(e)** $ _____	**(f)** $ _____	$648

Maguire Company
Budget Performance Report—Supervisor, Chip Fabrication
For the Month Ended May 31, 2014

Cost	Budget	Actual	Over Budget	Under Budget
Factory wages	$ 47,952	$ 49,200	$1,248	
Materials	125,280	124,416		$864
Power and light	6,912	8,208	1,296	
Maintenance	2,096	13,248	1,152	_____
	$192,240	$195,072	$3,696	$864

EXERCISE 24-1, Concluded

b. _____

_____

_____

_____

_____

_____

_____

_____

_____

_____

_____

_____

_____

_____

_____

_____

_____

_____

_____

_____

_____

_____

EXERCISE 24-2

Divisional Income Statements

	COMMERCIAL DIVISION	RESIDENTIAL DIVISION	

EXERCISE 24-3

a. Legal: _____

_____

b. Duplication services: _____

_____

c. Electronic data processing: _____

_____

d. Central purchasing: _____

_____

e. Telecommunications: _____

_____

f. Accounts receivable: _____

_____

EXERCISE 24-4

a. Conferences: _____

b. Telecommunications: _____

c. Accounts Receivable: _____

d. Payroll Accounting: _____

e. Employee Travel: _____

f. Central Purchasing: _____

g. Training: _____

h. Computer Support: _____

EXERCISE 24-5

a.

	RESIDENTIAL	COMMERCIAL	GOVERNMENT CONTRACT	TOTAL	

EXERCISE 24-5, Concluded

b.

	RESIDENTIAL	COMMERCIAL	GOVERNMENT CONTRACT	TOTAL

c. _____

EXERCISE 24-6

a. Help desk: _____

_____

_____

Network center: _____

_____

_____

Electronic mail: _____

_____

_____

Local voice support: _____

_____

_____

b. Help desk: _____

_____

_____

Network center: _____

_____

_____

Electronic mail: _____

_____

_____

Local voice support: _____

_____

_____

EXERCISE 24-7

Divisional Income Statements

	CONSUMER DIVISION		COMMERCIAL DIVISION	

Supporting calculations:

_____

_____

_____

_____

_____

_____

_____

_____

_____

EXERCISE 24-8

a. _____

_____

_____

_____

_____

_____

_____

_____

_____

_____

_____

_____

_____

_____

_____

_____

EXERCISE 24-8, Concluded

b.

	Divisional Income Statements			
	PASSENGER DIVISION		CARGO DIVISION	

Supporting calculations:

_____

_____

_____

_____

_____

_____

_____

_____

_____

_____

_____

_____

_____

_____

EXERCISE 24-9

Divisional Income Statements

	WINTER SPORTS DIVISION	SUMMER SPORTS DIVISION

EXERCISE 24-9, Concluded

Supporting Schedule:

_____

_____

_____

_____

_____

_____

_____

_____

_____

_____

_____

_____

_____

_____

_____

_____

_____

_____

_____

_____

EXERCISE 24-10

a. Retail Division: _____

Commercial Division: _____

Internet Division: _____

b. _____

EXERCISE 24-11

a.

	RETAIL DIVISION	COMMERCIAL DIVISION	INTERNET DIVISION

b. _____

EXERCISE 24-12

Rate of Return on Investment	=	Profit Margin	×	Investment Turnover
12%	=	5%	×	**(a)** _____
(b) _____	=	8%	×	2.00
14%	=	**(c)** _____	×	1.40
13.5%	=	6%	×	**(d)** _____
(e) _____	=	15%	×	1.20

EXERCISE 24-13

a. _____

_____

_____

_____

_____

_____

_____

_____

_____

_____

b. _____

_____

_____

_____

_____

_____

_____

_____

_____

_____

_____

_____

_____

_____

_____

_____

_____

EXERCISE 24-19

a. _____

b. _____

EXERCISE 24-20

a. _____

_____

_____

_____

_____

_____

_____

_____

b. _____

_____

_____

_____

_____

_____

_____

_____

c. _____

_____

_____

_____

_____

_____

_____

_____

EXERCISE 24-21

a. _____

_____

_____

_____

_____

_____

_____

_____

_____

_____

_____

b. _____

_____

_____

_____

_____

_____

_____

_____

_____

_____

_____

_____

_____

EXERCISE 24-21, Concluded

c. _____

_____

_____

_____

_____

_____

_____

_____

_____

_____

d. _____

_____

_____

_____

_____

_____

_____

_____

_____

_____

_____

PROBLEM 24-1 ___

1.

	BUDGET	ACTUAL	OVER BUDGET	UNDER BUDGET

Budget Performance Report — _____

2. _____

This Page Not Used.

PROBLEM 24-2 ___

1.

Divisional Income Statements			

Supporting schedule:

PROBLEM 24-2 ___, Concluded

2. _____

3. _____

PROBLEM 24-3 ___

1.

Divisional Income Statements

PROBLEM 24-3 ___, Continued

2. _____

_____

_____

_____

_____

_____

_____

_____

_____

_____

_____

_____

_____

_____

_____

_____

_____

_____

_____

_____

_____

_____

_____

_____

_____

_____

_____

_____

_____

_____

_____

_____

_____

_____

_____

_____

_____

PROBLEM 24-3 ___, Concluded

3. _____

_____

_____

_____

_____

_____

_____

_____

_____

_____

_____

_____

_____

This Page Not Used.

PROBLEM 24-4 ___

1. _____

_____

_____

_____

_____

_____

_____

_____

_____

_____

_____

_____

_____

_____

_____

_____

_____

_____

2.

_____

Estimated Income Statements

	PROPOSAL 1	PROPOSAL 2	PROPOSAL 3

PROBLEM 24-4 ___, Continued

3. _____

———

———

———

———

———

———

———

———

———

———

———

———

———

———

———

———

———

———

———

———

———

———

———

———

———

———

4. _____

———

———

PROBLEM 24-4 ___, Concluded

5. _____

_____

_____

_____

_____

_____

_____

_____

_____

_____

_____

_____

This Page Not Used.

PROBLEM 24-5 ___

1.

Divisional Income Statements		

PROBLEM 24-5 ___, Continued

2. _____

_____

_____

_____

_____

_____

_____

_____

_____

_____

_____

_____

_____

_____

_____

_____

_____

_____

_____

_____

_____

_____

_____

3. _____

_____

_____

_____

_____

PROBLEM 24-5 ___, Concluded

4. _____

_____

_____

_____

_____

_____

_____

_____

_____

_____

_____

_____

_____

_____

_____

_____

_____

_____

_____

_____

_____

_____

_____

_____

_____

_____

_____

This Page Not Used.

PROBLEM 24-6 ___

1. _____

   _____

   _____

   _____

   _____

PROBLEM 24-6 ___, Continued

2. _____

PROBLEM 24-6 ___, Continued

3.

	Divisional Income Statements		
			TOTAL

PROBLEM 24-6 ___, Continued

4. _____

_____

_____

_____

_____

_____

_____

_____

_____

_____

_____

_____

_____

_____

_____

_____

_____

_____

_____

_____

_____

_____

_____

_____

_____

_____

_____

_____

_____

_____

_____

_____

_____

_____

_____

_____

_____

PROBLEM 24-6 ___, Concluded

5. a. _____

_____

_____

_____

_____

b. _____

_____

_____

_____

_____

This Page Not Used.

EXERCISE 25-1   1, 2, 7, 12, 15, 16, 18, 20

a.

Lease Machinery (Alternative 1) or Sell Machinery (Alternative 2)

	LEASE MACHINERY (ALTERNATIVE 1)	SELL MACHINERY (ALTERNATIVE 2)	DIFFERENTIAL EFFECT ON INCOME (ALTERNATIVE 2)

b. _____

_____

EXERCISE 25-2

Lease Equipment (Alternative 1) or Buy Equipment (Alternative 2)

	LEASE EQUIPMENT (ALTERNATIVE 1)	BUY EQUIPMENT (ALTERNATIVE 2)	DIFFERENTIAL EFFECT ON INCOME (ALTERNATIVE 2)

EXERCISE 25-3

a.

	Continue Star Cola (Alternative 1) or Discontinue Star Cola (Alternative 2)		

	CONTINUE STAR COLA (ALTERNATIVE 1)	DISCONTINUE STAR COLA (ALTERNATIVE 2)	DIFFERENTIAL EFFECT ON INCOME (ALTERNATIVE 2)

b. _____

_____

_____

EXERCISE 25-4

a.

	Continue Cups (Alternative 1) or Discontinue Cups (Alternative 2)		
	CONTINUE CUPS (ALTERNATIVE 1)	DISCONTINUE CUPS (ALTERNATIVE 2)	DIFFERENTIAL EFFECT ON INCOME (ALTERNATIVE 2)

b. _____

_____

_____

EXERCISE 25-5

a. _____

_____

_____

_____

_____

_____

_____

_____

b. _____

_____

_____

_____

_____

_____

_____

_____

_____

_____

_____

_____

_____

_____

_____

_____

_____

_____

_____

_____

_____

c.

	INVESTOR SERVICES (IN MILLIONS)	INSTITUTIONAL SERVICES (IN MILLIONS)

EXERCISE 25-5, Concluded

d. _____

_____

_____

_____

_____

_____

_____

_____

_____

_____

_____

EXERCISE 25-6

_____

_____

_____

_____

_____

_____

_____

_____

_____

Continue Children's Shoes (Alternative 1) or Discontinue Children's Shoes (Alternative 2)

	CONTINUE CHILDREN'S SHOES (ALTERNATIVE 1)	DISCONTINUE CHILDREN'S SHOES (ALTERNATIVE 2)	DIFFERENTIAL EFFECT ON INCOME (ALTERNATIVE 2)

EXERCISE 25-7

a.

Make Carrying Case (Alternative 1) or Buy Carrying Case (Alternative 2)

	MAKE CARRYING CASE (ALTERNATIVE 1)	BUY CARRYING CASE (ALTERNATIVE 2)	DIFFERENTIAL EFFECT ON INCOME (ALTERNATIVE 2)

b. _____

_____

_____

_____

_____

_____

_____

EXERCISE 25-8

a.

Lay Out Pages Internally (Alternative 1) or Purchase Layout Services (Alternative 2)			
	LAY OUT PAGES INTERNALLY (ALTERNATIVE 1)	PURCHASE LAYOUT SERVICES (ALTERNATIVE 2)	DIFFERENTIAL EFFECT ON INCOME (ALTERNATIVE 2)

b. _____

EXERCISE 25-8, Concluded

c. _____

_____

_____

_____

_____

_____

_____

_____

_____

_____

_____

_____

EXERCISE 25-9

a.

| | | Continue with Old Machine (Alternative 1) or Replace Old Machine (Alternative 2) | | |

	CONTINUE WITH OLD MACHINE (ALTERNATIVE 1)	REPLACE OLD MACHINE (ALTERNATIVE 2)	DIFFERENTIAL EFFECT ON INCOME (ALTERNATIVE 2)

b. _____

_____

_____

_____

EXERCISE 25-10

a.

	Continue with Old Machine (Alternative 1) or Replace Old Machine (Alternative 2)		
	CONTINUE WITH OLD MACHINE (ALTERNATIVE 1)	REPLACE OLD MACHINE (ALTERNATIVE 2)	DIFFERENTIAL EFFECT ON INCOME (ALTERNATIVE 2)

b. _____

_____

c. _____

_____

_____

_____

_____

_____

_____

_____

_____

_____

EXERCISE 25-11

Sell Rough Cut (Alternative 1) or Process Further into Finished Cut (Alternative 2)

	SELL ROUGH CUT (ALTERNATIVE 1)	PROCESS FURTHER INTO FINISHED CUT (ALTERNATIVE 2)	DIFFERENTIAL EFFECT ON INCOME (ALTERNATIVE 2)

EXERCISE 25-12

a.

Sell Regular Columbian (Alternative 1) or Process Further into Decaf Columbian (Alternative 2)

	SELL REGULAR COLUMBIAN (ALTERNATIVE 1)	PROCESS FURTHER INTO DECAF COLUMBIAN (ALTERNATIVE 2)	DIFFERENTIAL EFFECT ON INCOME (ALTERNATIVE 2)

b. _____

EXERCISE 25-12, Concluded

c. _____

_____
_____
_____
_____
_____
_____
_____
_____
_____
_____
_____
_____
_____
_____
_____
_____
_____
_____
_____
_____

Sell Regular Columbian (Alternative 1) or Process Further into Decaf Columbian (Alternative 2)

	SELL REGULAR COLUMBIAN (ALTERNATIVE 1)	PROCESS FURTHER INTO DECAF COLUMBIAN (ALTERNATIVE 2)	DIFFERENTIAL EFFECT ON INCOME (ALTERNATIVE 2)

EXERCISE 25-13

a.

	Reject Order (Alternative 1) or Accept Order (Alternative 2)		
	REJECT ORDER (ALTERNATIVE 1)	ACCEPT ORDER (ALTERNATIVE 2)	DIFFERENTIAL EFFECT ON INCOME (ALTERNATIVE 2)

b. _____

c. _____

EXERCISE 25-14

EXERCISE 25-15

a.

Reject Order (Alternative 1) or Accept Order (Alternative 2)			
	REJECT ORDER (ALTERNATIVE 1)	ACCEPT ORDER (ALTERNATIVE 2)	DIFFERENTIAL EFFECT ON INCOME (ALTERNATIVE 2)

b. _____

_____

_____

_____

_____

EXERCISE 25-16

a. _____

b. _____

_____

c. _____

_____

_____

_____

_____

_____

_____

_____

_____

d.

EXERCISE 25-17

a. _____

b. _____

_____

c. _____

_____

_____

_____

_____

_____

_____

_____

_____

_____

_____

_____

_____

EXERCISE 25-17, Concluded

d.

EXERCISE 25-18

a. _____

_____

_____

_____

_____

b. _____

_____

_____

_____

_____

_____

_____

_____

_____

_____

_____

_____

_____

EXERCISE 25-19

a.

b.

c.

EXERCISE 25-20

	TYPE 5	TYPE 10	TYPE 20

EXERCISE 25-21

a.

	LARGE	MEDIUM	SMALL	TOTAL

b. _____

_____

	LARGE	MEDIUM	SMALL

EXERCISE 25-22

	A	B	C	D	E	F	G	H	I	J	K	L
1				Stationary Bicycle						Treadmill		
2			—	—	=	Activity		—	—	=		Activity
3	Activity		—	—		Cost		—	—			Cost
4												
5												
6												
7												
8												
9												
10												
11												
12												
13												
14												
15												

EXERCISE 25-23

a.

	PRODUCTION SETUP	PROCUREMENT	QUALITY CONTROL	MATERIALS MANAGEMENT

b.

	CUSTOM		STANDARD	

EXERCISE 25-23, Concluded

c. _____

_____

_____

_____

_____

_____

_____

_____

_____

_____

_____

d. _____

_____

_____

_____

_____

_____

_____

_____

_____

_____

_____

_____

_____

EXERCISE 25-24

a.

	A	B	C	D	E	F
1						Activity
2	Activity		—	—	=	Rate
3						
4						
5						
6						
7						
8						
9						
10						

b.

	A	B	C	D	E	F	G	H	I	J	K	L
1			Entry Lighting Fixtures					Dining Room Lighting Fixtures			
2						Activity						Activity
3	Activity		—	—	=	Cost		—	—	=		Cost
4												
5												
6												
7												
8												
9												
10												
11												
12												
13												
14												
15												

APPENDIX EXERCISE 25-25

a.

b.

c.

APPENDIX EXERCISE 25-26

a.

b.

c.

PROBLEM 25-1 ___

1.

_____

Operate _____ *(Alternative 1) or Invest in Bonds (Alternative 2)*

	OPERATE _____ _____ (ALTERNATIVE 1)	INVEST IN BONDS (ALTERNATIVE 2)	DIFFERENTIAL EFFECT ON INCOME (ALTERNATIVE 2)

2. _____

_____

3.

This Page Not Used.

PROBLEM 25-2 ___

1.

	CONTINUE WITH OLD MACHINE (ALTERNATIVE 1)	REPLACE OLD MACHINE (ALTERNATIVE 2)	DIFFERENTIAL EFFECT ON INCOME (ALTERNATIVE 2)
Continue with Old Machine (Alternative 1) or Replace Old Machine (Alternative 2)			

PROBLEM 25-2 ___, Concluded

2. _____

_____

_____

_____

_____

_____

_____

_____

_____

_____

_____

_____

_____

_____

_____

_____

_____

_____

_____

_____

_____

_____

_____

_____

PROBLEM 25-3 ___

1.

_____

_____ *Promote _____ (Alternative 1) or Promote _____ (Alternative 2)*

	PROMOTE _____ (ALTERNATIVE 1)	PROMOTE _____ (ALTERNATIVE 2)	DIFFERENTIAL EFFECT ON INCOME (ALTERNATIVE 2)	

_____

_____

2. _____

_____

_____

_____

_____

_____

_____

_____

_____

_____

_____

This Page Not Used.

PROBLEM 25-4 ___

1.

_Sell _____ (Alternative 1) or Process Further into _____ (Alternative 2)_

	SELL _____ (ALTERNATIVE 1)	PROCESS FURTHER INTO _____ (ALTERNATIVE 2)	DIFFERENTIAL EFFECT ON INCOME (ALTERNATIVE 2)

2. _____

_____

_____

_____

_____

This Page Not Used.

PROBLEM 25-5 ___

1. _____

2. a.

b.

c.

PROBLEM 25-5 ___ , Continued

3. (APPENDIX)

   a.

   b.

   c.

PROBLEM 25-5 ___, Continued

4. (APPENDIX)

a. _____

_____

_____

b. _____

_____

_____

_____

_____

_____

_____

_____

_____

_____

c.

5. _____

_____

_____

_____

_____

_____

_____

PROBLEM 25-5 ___ , Concluded

6. a.

Reject Order (Alternative 1) or Accept Order (Alternative 2)

	REJECT ORDER (ALTERNATIVE 1)	ACCEPT ORDER (ALTERNATIVE 2)	DIFFERENTIAL EFFECT ON INCOME (ALTERNATIVE 2)

b. _____

_____

PROBLEM 25-6 ___

1.

PROBLEM 25-6 ___, Concluded

2.

Explanation:

_____
_____
_____
_____
_____
_____
_____
_____
_____
_____
_____
_____
_____
_____
_____
_____

PROBLEM 25-7 ___

1.

Name _____

PROBLEM 25-7 _____, Continued

2.

	A	B	C	D	E	F	G	H	I	J	K	L
1												
2	Activity		—	=	Activity Cost			—			=	Activity Cost
3												
4												
5												
6												
7												
8												
9												
10												
11												
12												
13												
14												
15												

	A	B	C	D	E	F
1						
2	Activity		—	=	Activity Cost
3						
4						
5						
6						
7						
8						
9						
10						
11						
12						
13						
14						
15						

PROBLEM 25-7 ___, Concluded

3. _____

_____

_____

_____

_____

_____

_____

_____

_____

_____

_____

_____

This Page Not Used.

EXERCISE 26-1

	TESTING EQUIPMENT	VEHICLE	

EXERCISE 26-2

_____

_____

_____

_____

_____

_____

_____

_____

_____

_____

_____

_____

_____

_____

_____

_____

EXERCISE 26-3

	YEAR 1	YEARS 2–9	LAST YEAR

EXERCISE 26-4

	YEAR 1	YEARS 2–9	LAST YEAR

EXERCISE 26-5

_____

_____

	NET CASH FLOW	CUMULATIVE NET CASH FLOWS

EXERCISE 26-6

a. _____

_____

_____

_____

_____

_____

	LIQUID SOAP		BODY LOTION	
	NET CASH FLOW	CUMULATIVE NET CASH FLOWS	NET CASH FLOW	CUMULATIVE NET CASH FLOWS

_____

EXERCISE 26-6, Concluded

b. _____

_____

_____

_____

_____

_____

_____

_____

_____

_____

_____

_____

_____

_____

_____

_____

_____

EXERCISE 26-7

a.

Year	Present Value of $1 at 15%	Net Cash Flow	Present Value of Net Cash Flow
1			
2			
3			
4			
Total...			
Less amount to be invested...			
Net present value			

b. _____

_____

EXERCISE 26-8

a.

	2014	2015	2016	2017	2018

b.

Year	Net Cash Flow [from part a.]	Present Value of $1 at 12%	Present Value of Net Cash Flow
2014			
2015			
2016			
2017			
2018			
Total present value of cash flows			
Less investment in delivery truck			
Net present value of delivery truck...			

c. _____

_____

_____

_____

_____

_____

EXERCISE 26-9

a.

	(IN MILLIONS)	

EXERCISE 26-9, Concluded

b.

	(IN MILLIONS, EXCEPT PRESENT VALUE FACTOR)

c. _____

_____

_____

_____

_____

_____

EXERCISE 26-10

a.

EXERCISE 26-10, Concluded

b.

c. _____

_____

_____

_____

d. _____

_____

_____

_____

_____

_____

_____

_____

EXERCISE 26-11

a.

b.

EXERCISE 26-12

a.

b.

EXERCISE 26-13

a. _____

Sewing Machine:

Packing Machine:

b. _____

EXERCISE 26-13, Concluded

c. _____

_____

_____

_____

_____

_____

_____

_____

_____

_____

_____

_____

_____

_____

_____

_____

_____

_____

_____

_____

EXERCISE 26-14

a. _____

_____

_____

_____

b. _____

_____

_____

c.

EXERCISE 26-15

a. _____

_____

_____

b. _____

_____

_____

_____

c. _____

_____

_____

_____

_____

_____

_____

_____

_____

_____

_____

_____

_____

_____

_____

_____

_____

_____

_____

_____

_____

EXERCISE 26-16

a. _____

_____

_____

_____

_____

_____

_____

b. _____

_____

EXERCISE 26-17

a. _____

b. _____

EXERCISE 26-18

a. Delivery Truck:

Bagging Machine:

EXERCISE 26-18, Concluded

b. _____

_____

_____

_____

_____

_____

_____

_____

_____

_____

_____

_____

_____

EXERCISE 26-19

a.

b. _____

c. _____

_____

_____

_____

_____

_____

_____

_____

_____

_____

EXERCISE 26-20

EXERCISE 26-21

Processing Mill:

Year	Present Value of $1 at 15%	Net Cash Flow	Present Value of Net Cash Flow
1			
2			
3			
4			
4 (residual value)			
Total..			
Less amount to be invested			
Net present value			

Electric Shovel:

Year	Present Value of $1 at 15%	Net Cash Flow	Present Value of Net Cash Flow
1			
2			
3			
4			
Total..			
Less amount to be invested			
Net present value			

Conclusion with explanation:

_____

_____

_____

_____

_____

_____

_____

EXERCISE 26-22

a. Blending Equipment:

Computer System:

b. _____

PROBLEM 26-1 ___

1. a. _____

_____

_____

_____

_____

_____

_____

b.

Year	Present Value of $1 at _____%	Net Cash Flow		Present Value of Net Cash Flow	
		Project: _____ _____	Project: _____ _____	Project: _____ _____	Project: _____ _____
1					
2					
3					
4					
5					
Total............................					
Less amount to be invested				
Net present value				

2. _____

_____

_____

_____

_____

_____

_____

_____

_____

_____

_____

_____

_____

_____

_____

_____

_____

This Page Not Used.

PROBLEM 26-2 ___

1. a.

Year	Net Cash Flow	Cumulative Net Cash Flow

Year	Net Cash Flow	Cumulative Net Cash Flow

b.

Year	Present Value of $1 at _____%	Net Cash Flow		Present Value of Net Cash Flow	
		Project (Product): _____ _____	Project (Product): _____ _____	Project (Product): _____ _____	Project (Product): _____ _____
1					
2					
3					
4					
5					
Total............................					
Less amount to be invested				
Net present value				

PROBLEM 26-2 ___, Concluded

2. _____

_____

_____

_____

_____

_____

_____

_____

_____

_____

_____

_____

_____

_____

_____

_____

_____

_____

_____

PROBLEM 26-3 ___

1. Proposal (Project): _____

Year	Present Value of $1 at _____%	Net Cash Flow	Present Value of Net Cash Flow
1			
2			
3			
Total..			
Less amount to be invested			
Net present value			

Proposal (Project): _____

Year	Present Value of $1 at _____%	Net Cash Flow	Present Value of Net Cash Flow
1			
2			
3			
Total..			
Less amount to be invested			
Net present value			

Proposal (Project): _____

Year	Present Value of $1 at _____%	Net Cash Flow	Present Value of Net Cash Flow
1			
2			
3			
Total..			
Less amount to be invested			
Net present value			

PROBLEM 26-3 ___, Concluded

2. _____

3. _____

PROBLEM 26-4 ___

1. a. Project: _____

Project: _____

b. _____

_____

_____

_____

_____

_____

_____

_____

_____

_____

PROBLEM 26-4 ___, Concluded

2. a. _____

_____

_____

_____

_____

_____

_____

_____

_____

_____

b. _____

_____

_____

_____

3. _____

_____

_____

_____

_____

_____

_____

_____

_____

_____

_____

_____

_____

_____

_____

_____

_____

_____

PROBLEM 26-5 ___

1. Project (Site): _____

Project (Site): _____

2.

Year	Present Value of $1 at ____%	Net Cash Flow		Present Value of Net Cash Flow	
		Project (Site): _____	Project (Site): _____	Project (Site): _____	Project (Site): _____
1					
2					
3					
4					
4 (residual value)					
Total					
Less amount to be invested..					
Net present value...					

PROBLEM 26-5 ___, Concluded

3. _____

_____

_____

_____

_____

_____

_____

_____

_____

_____

_____

_____

_____

_____

_____

_____

_____

PROBLEM 26-6 ___

1. Proposal A:

Year	Net Cash Flow	Cumulative Net Cash Flows

Proposal B:

Year	Net Cash Flow	Cumulative Net Cash Flows

Proposal C:

Year	Net Cash Flow	Cumulative Net Cash Flows

Proposal D:

Year	Net Cash Flow	Cumulative Net Cash Flows

PROBLEM 26-6 ___, Continued

2. Proposal A: _____

_____

_____

_____

_____

_____

Proposal B: _____

_____

_____

_____

_____

_____

Proposal C: _____

_____

_____

_____

_____

_____

Proposal D: _____

_____

_____

_____

_____

_____

PROBLEM 26-6 ___, Continued

3.

Proposal	Cash Payback Period	Average Rate of Return	Accept for Further Analysis	Reject
A				
B				
C				
D				

4. Proposal ___:

Year	Present Value of $1 at _____%	Net Cash Flow	Present Value of Net Cash Flow
1			
2			
3			
4			
5			
Total..		
Less amount to be invested		
Net present value		

Proposal ___:

Year	Present Value of $1 at _____%	Net Cash Flow	Present Value of Net Cash Flow
1			
2			
3			
4			
5			
Total..		
Less amount to be invested		
Net present value		

PROBLEM 26-6 ___, Concluded

5. _____

6. _____

7. _____

8. _____

EXTRA FORMS
JOURNAL

PAGE

	DATE		DESCRIPTION	POST. REF.	DEBIT	CREDIT	
1							1
2							2
3							3
4							4
5							5
6							6
7							7
8							8
9							9
10							10
11							11
12							12
13							13
14							14
15							15
16							16
17							17
18							18
19							19
20							20
21							21
22							22
23							23
24							24
25							25
26							26
27							27
28							28
29							29
30							30
31							31
32							32
33							33
34							34
35							35
36							36

EXTRA FORMS

JOURNAL

PAGE

	DATE		DESCRIPTION	POST. REF.	DEBIT	CREDIT	
1							1
2							2
3							3
4							4
5							5
6							6
7							7
8							8
9							9
10							10
11							11
12							12
13							13
14							14
15							15
16							16
17							17
18							18
19							19
20							20
21							21
22							22
23							23
24							24
25							25
26							26
27							27
28							28
29							29
30							30
31							31
32							32
33							33
34							34
35							35
36							36

EXTRA FORMS

JOURNAL

PAGE

	DATE		DESCRIPTION	POST. REF.	DEBIT	CREDIT	
1							1
2							2
3							3
4							4
5							5
6							6
7							7
8							8
9							9
10							10
11							11
12							12
13							13
14							14
15							15
16							16
17							17
18							18
19							19
20							20
21							21
22							22
23							23
24							24
25							25
26							26
27							27
28							28
29							29
30							30
31							31
32							32
33							33
34							34
35							35
36							36

EXTRA FORMS

number of times interest charges earned =  ...come tax + interest exp

...rest expense

EXTRA FORMS

14-22

                                                         MKt = 8%   N = 8

Sales Price = Present Value of Bond → MKt rate   Stated = 10%   i = 8% → 4%

① Calculate Present Value of Face Amount
30,000,000 × .73069 = 21,920,700

                     +   Interest = face × rate × time

② Calculate Present Value of int PMT   30,000,000 × 10% × 6/12
1,500,000 × 6.73274 = 10,099,110   = 1,500,000
                  32,019,810 = cash

① Sell Bond

Cash	32,019,810	
Bonds Payable (Face amount)		30,000,000
premium on Bonds Payable		2,019,810

② Pay Interest expense

Int. Expense	1,247,523.75	
Prem on BP	252,476.25	
Cash		1,500,000

③ Pay Bond off at Maturity

Bonds Payable	30,000,000	
Cash		30,000,000

EXTRA FORMS

Adj Entry

Dec 31   Valuation allowance for Trading Securities   25,000
              Unrecognized Gain or loss   25,

Available for Sale

     Valuation allowance for (Available 9 Sale)   25,000
        Unrecognized Gain or loss   25,000

                   Investments (Asset)

Short term ←   → Long term
Trading securities   Debt → hold to Maturity
Available for Sale securities

                      equity (Stock)
                      < 20% → Cost Method
                      > 20% → Equity Method
                      > 50% → Consolidate

Ch 15

   Inv in Bonds   12000
      Cash   12000

   Cash   1000
   Investmen in Bonds   300
     Interest Revenue   1300

   Cash   15000
     Investment in Bonds